PUBLIC EXECUTIONS

PUBLIC EXECUTIONS

NIGEL CAWTHORNE

CHARTWELL
BOOKS, INC.

This edition printed in 2006 by

CHARTWELL BOOKS, INC.
A Division of **BOOK SALES, INC.**
114 Northfield Avenue
Edison, New Jersey 08837

Copyright © 2006 Arcturus Publishing Limited
26/27 Bickels Yard, 151–153 Bermondsey Street,
London SE1 3HA

ISBN-13: 978-0-7858-2119-9
ISBN-10: 0-7858-2119-8

Printed in China

Picture Credits
Art Archive/Picture Desk: 11, 13, 30, 56, 68, 75, 143
AKG: 21, 67, 158
Corbis: 52, 142, 162, 167, 169, 175, 179, 202, 203
Getty Images: 14, 47, 76, 86, 97, 117, 137, 164, 171, 194, 198
Mary Evans: 18, 24, 28, 34, 37, 38, 40, 42, 44, 78, 81, 82, 85,87, 89, 90,
101, 102, 104, 106, 108, 111, 112, 120, 127, 128, 134, 136, 133, 145,
146, 149, 150, 152, 154, 163, 172, 183 184, 189, 191, 200
Topham Picturepoint: 23, 62, 79, 95

Contents

Introduction

In Britain and the United States, public execution was outlawed in 1868 and in 1936 respectively. However, it is still practised in many countries around the world. These include Iran, Saudi Arabia, China and, some would argue, the United States, where large numbers of witnesses are invited to view the demise of condemned criminals. Most civilized countries, however, view public execution with distaste.

This is, however, a very modern view. In earlier times, an execution behind closed doors was regarded as little more than murder. It robbed the victim of the opportunity to make his final speech from the scaffold and certainly deprived the State of the chance to parade its power before those who fell under its jurisdiction, be they criminals, enemies, or political opponents. Above all, the public missed out on what was considered a great spectacle – Christians thrown to the lions in Rome's Colosseum, multiple hangings at Tyburn, guillotined aristocrats at the Place de la Concorde, heretics burned alive at the *auto-da-fé* or the still-pulsating hearts ripped from the chests of war prisoners by Aztec priests at the summit of their temple pyramids.

The theatre of public execution offered further political gains. When Charles I was beheaded, the block was only ten inches high rather than the conventional two feet. This meant he could not kneel for his execution but was forced to lie face down, a position considered by his executioners to be more humiliating.

Beheading was one of the most common methods used in public execution, and it did at least have the virtue – from the victim's point of view – of being quick. There was also death by beating, boiling, breaking on a wheel, burning, crucifixion, drowning, hanging, keel-hauling, necklacing (officially sanctioned in Haiti), starvation in a cage, stoning, strangulation or a thousand cuts; by being buried alive, devoured by animals, exposed on a gibbet, fried on a gridiron, garrotted, guillotined, hammered to death, hanged, drawn and quartered, impaled on a stake, rent asunder between two trees, roasted alive, sat on the 'Spanish donkey', sawn in half, sealed up in a barrel, sewn inside an animal's stomach, shot at with arrows, stung to death by insects, tied to a mill wheel or a sack filled with animals, tied over the muzzle of a cannon and blown apart, thrown from a height, torn apart between two boats; by having gunpowder ignited through bodily orifices, your heart torn out or your throat slit.

Public executions not only despatched the victims but also brutalized

executioners and spectators alike. The Romans, who purposefully pitted inadequate criminals or defenceless Christians against mighty gladiators, saw an advantage in this. They believed public execution taught onlookers to confront death.

No such noble excuse could be made for the huge crowds that gathered along Oxford Road (London's Oxford Street) to see condemned prisoners being taken from Newgate Prison to Tyburn. Popular offenders were showered with flowers and unpopular ones pelted with rotten vegetables or stones. Around the gallows at Tyburn were wooden stands where spectators paid two shillings – 10p – for a good view. The largest and most desirable stand was Old Mother Proctor's Pews, named after their owner. The whole affair had a carnival feel about it with crowds singing and chanting, and street vendors selling gingerbread, gin, and oranges. There was certainly nothing noble about dying in these places.

C H A P T E R   1

The Roman Way of Death

In ancient Rome, death was dictated by social class. At one end, the patricians and the equestrians were allowed to poison themselves in private. At the other, slaves were publicly crucified. Although this form of public execution is now associated with the death of Jesus Christ, it was a common form of capital punishment when the Roman Empire was at its height. Crucifixion was not invented by the Romans – there are mentions of it in earlier Greek literature – although they seem to have perfected the practice. Herodotus, the father of ancient history, who lived in the fifth century BC, recorded that the Persian King Darius I ordered the crucifixion of 3,000 Babylonians in about 519 BC.

Crucifixion

When Alexander the Great attacked the Persian Empire in the fourth century BC, he crucified 2,000 men from the Phoenician city of Tyre (modern-day Sur in southern Lebanon) along the beach after the city refused him worship in their temple and forced him into a costly siege. The Romans learned about crucifixion from the Greeks, although they noted that many of the 'barbarian' races (Indians, Assyrians, Scythians, and Celts) also used it. The Carthaginians employed crucifixion until Carthage was destroyed by the Romans in 146 BC.

Some Romans regarded crucifixion as uncivilized. In the first century BC, the statesman Cicero called it 'the most cruel and disgusting penalty' and considered it the worst of deaths. The Jewish historian Joseph Ben Matthias (aka Flavius Josephus), who witnessed numerous crucifixions during the Jewish revolt in AD 66–70, called it 'the most wretched of deaths'.

The first-century Roman philosopher Lucius Annaeus Seneca asked: 'Can anyone be found who would prefer wasting away in pain dying limb-by-limb, or letting out his life drop-by-drop, rather than expiring once [and] for all? Can any man be found willing to be fastened to the accursed tree, long sickly, already deformed, swelling with ugly wounds on shoulders and chest, and drawing the breath of life amid long, drawn-out agony? He would have many excuses for dying even before mounting the cross.'

The respected third-century Roman jurist Julius Paulus also considered crucifixion to be the worst of all capital punishments. When listing various methods, he put it ahead of death by burning, beheading, or being eaten by wild beasts. It was obviously not viewed as a normal death sentence : in Roman eyes, crucifixion was humiliating, disgraceful, and obscene.

In most circumstances, the law spared Roman citizens from the degradation of crucifixion but it was widely used against rebellious foreigners, enemies, thieves, criminals, and slaves. Slaves were indeed crucified so routinely that it became known as the *servile supplicium* or 'slaves' punishment'. When Spartacus' slave rebellion was crushed in 71 BC, the victorious Roman general Crassus crucified 6,000 slaves along the Appian Way, the main road leading into Rome from the south. As the Roman general and later emperor Titus was putting down the Jewish revolt and beginning the siege of Jerusalem in AD 70, he was at one point also crucifying over 500 Jews a day. Josephus, in his *History of the Jewish Wars,* claimed that so many Jews were crucified outside the city walls 'there was not enough room for the crosses and not enough crosses for the bodies'. By the time the siege was over, there were no trees left within twelve miles of the city limits.

It is believed that the first crucified victims were simply nailed to a tree. Several different methods were later developed but the Romans standardized the procedure: their guiding principle was to inflict the maximum pain and indignity on the person being punished.

Firstly, the prisoner would be stripped and his hands tied to a post as two soldiers proceeded to administer a public flogging. A short whip with leather thongs of different lengths known as a *flagrum* or *flagellum* was used. Fixed to the ends of these thongs were sharp shards of sheep bone or small iron balls, which cut into the flesh. The victim's back, buttocks, and legs would be scourged and the beating would only cease when he passed out. There would be much shedding of blood and some individuals would not even survive the flogging. If they did, considerable blood loss ensured that they died more swiftly on the cross. The flagellation of Jesus must have been particularly brutal, since he died only six hours after being crucified.

The condemned person was made to carry his cross as part of a public procession to the place of crucifixion outside the city walls. It was usually sited on high ground, so that the spectacle could be seen by the maximum number of people, and it would be near a road, to serve as a warning to passers-by. To further emphasize the point, the bodies of victims were often left to rot until only the skeletons remained. Rome's place of crucifixion was on the Campus Esquilinus, and Jerusalem had Golgotha.

The victim would not have been forced to carry the whole cross himself because it could weigh over 300 pounds. The *stipes* (vertical posts) were a permanent installation at Campus Esquilinus, Golgotha, and their equivalents so only the *patibulum* (cross-piece) would actually be carried by the prisoner. It would have weighed between 75 and 125 pounds. Carrying it would have been agony as the rough wood of the *patibulum* was placed across the shoulders where the flesh had been lacerated by flogging.

The procession to the crucifixion site was flanked by military guards and headed by a centurion. A sign or *titulus* outlining the person's crimes was slung around his neck or carried by a soldier. This sign would later be nailed to the top of the cross. The *titulus* on Jesus' cross simply declared that he was 'the King of the Jews'.

On the Cross

When prisoners reached their place of execution, they had to be given a drink of wine mixed with myrrh known as *galla*. This mild narcotic would help deaden the pain. The naked individual would be made to lie down on his back with his arms outstretched along the cross-piece. His hands would either be tied or nailed to the wood. The Romans preferred nailing even though this meant that the victim expired more quickly. Seven-inch iron nails were hammered through the palms or, more commonly, the wrists as this provided better support for the weight of the body. The cross-piece was winched into position and tied or nailed to the upright while iron nails were driven through the insteps or soles to secure the feet. If the victim was being crucified on a site without permanent uprights, the cross would be assembled flat on the ground and the victim nailed to it. The whole structure would then be hoisted vertically and the base of the upright dropped into a socket in the ground and fixed into position with wedges.

As there was the genuine risk that a victim's hands or wrists could pull away from the nails, allowing the body to slump forward, a block of wood or plank was fixed to the upright to take some of the weight. This piece of wood was either a *sedile* (which the victim straddled) or a *suppedanem* (which he stood on).

Some individuals were crucified on tall crosses although shorter crosses – no more than seven feet high – were more common. Despite the depiction

of tall crosses in classical art, it seems that Jesus was crucified on the shorter version. According to the Bible, a Roman soldier impaled a sponge soaked in wine on the end of a hyssop plant stalk – typically eighteen inches long – to give to Jesus to drink. Had it been a tall cross, the stalk would not have reached his mouth.

The pain was excruciating. The scourging and hammering of nails through the flesh was bad enough, but once the cross had been erected, the victim would suffer the agony of his body weight pulling on the nails. The position of the arms lifted up his chest, which would have made proper breathing impossible unless he raised his body by turning in his elbows and

Right: Christ on the Cross. The Roman statesman Cicero called crucifixion 'the most cruel and disgusting penalty; the worst of deaths'

pushed up with his feet. As well as causing searing pain to both hands and feet, the movement would have rubbed the man's scourged back up the rough shaft of the wooden cross. Every breath was agony and the shortage of oxygen in the bloodstream produced painful muscular cramps. As if these torments were not enough, victims were also beaten with hooked instruments or had honey rubbed on their faces to attract insects. They eventually died of exhaustion and asphyxiation.

There were other ways in which crucified people were despatched. Sometimes a sharp weapon was forced up the rectum or a lance was used to pierce the side, as in the case of Jesus. The head was often scalped and the genitals removed. Red-hot pokers were thrust down the victim's throat or into his eyes. The body could be dowsed with oil and faggots piled around the foot of the cross and set alight, turning victim and cross into a blazing torch.

The two thieves crucified with Jesus – traditionally known as Dismas and Gestas – had their legs broken to speed up their dying. This gesture was not made out of compassion: the Roman authorities simply did not want the bodies hanging there on the next day, which was a holiday. Jesus, too, would have had his legs broken but he was already dead.

Normally death did not come so quickly. A healthy person could survive on the cross for one or two days. The naked man would be jeered at and ridiculed. Insects would infest his mouth, eyes, and open wounds. With his hands nailed to the cross, he would have been unable to stop them. Left to the elements, unable to eat or drink, in constant pain, and brutally aware he was going to die, there can be no doubt that, as the ancients tell us, crucifixion was the worst of deaths.

Some people miraculously survived. There was one account of a man who claimed to have been cut down and rescued by friends. He recalled the lines of jeering people that lined the route as he carried the *patibulum* to the place of crucifixion. He was stripped and left 'with not even covering for my private parts, which were much ogled by coarse women, I thought, and peered at by men'. The six mallet blows that nailed his palms to the cross-piece left him sweating and trembling. A single nail pinned both of his feet and he could hear the bone splintering. Distracted by the pain in his arms, he still felt 'a thousand fires shoot up my legs, invade my thighs and loins, and penetrate deep into my stomach'.

The agony grew more intense as the cross was raised. He felt the nails tearing through the flesh of his hands and feet, and longed for a rope around his waist to relieve the heaviness of his body. Weakening, he sagged forward, which increased the pain and made him wish that a spear might be thrust in his side to pierce his heart and end his misery.

He did not know how long he hung there but felt all his blood draining from his body. The drip, drip, drip of it seemed to ring in his ears. Suddenly he remembered the world turning upside down as the cross was taken down. There was renewed pain in his hands and feet as the nails were removed but he managed to stumble into a nearby wood where friends found him three days later. This account, however, must be taken with a pinch of salt: the victim was a devout Christian and it is something of a coincidence that Jesus himself was resurrected after just three days.

Dismas, the repentant thief at Jesus' side, became the patron saint of the condemned. A piece of the cross upon which he died is said to be preserved in the Church of Santa Croce in Rome. The cross upon which Jesus was crucified – the 'True Cross' – was supposed to have been found by Saint Helena, Emperor Constantine's mother, on her trip to the Holy Land in 326. It was later thought to have been destroyed by Saladdin but fragments still circulated around Europe. Put together, however, these pieces would have made up far more than just one cross! One piece was brought to Scotland from Hungary by Saint Margaret, wife of Malcolm III, and housed in the Abbey at Dunfermline. Known as the Black Rood, it was later seized by the English who took it to Durham, where it was later lost.

Variations of Crucifixion

Although the Romans had crucifixion down to a fine art, there were variations. In his *Dialogues* Seneca states, 'I see crosses there, not just of one kind but made in many different ways: some have their victims with heads down to the ground; some impale their private parts; others stretch out their arms on the gibbet'.

The Romans devised the *crux immissa* with two cross-pieces set at right angles. Four victims could be crucified together, with weights tied to their feet. A variation of this was the *crux commissa* which had three arms. There was another device that resembled soccer goal posts, where two offenders could be nailed up by one arm and one leg each, and there was the *crux decussata* or St Andrew's Cross, on which the victim was spread-eagled and mutilated. According to Seneca, when people were crucified upside down it was more merciful, because the victim soon lost consciousness.

Although crucifixion was banned in 345 by Constantine, Rome's first Christian emperor, the practice continued in the more barbaric provinces. In France, the assassin Bertholde, who killed Charles the Good, was crucified in 1127 on the orders of Louis the Fat. There are records from the thirteenth century of a religious fervour in England, where men declared themselves to be Christ and were duly crucified. In nineteenth-century Japan, victims were tied to crosses and slowly impaled with narrow spears. If a substantial bribe was paid beforehand, the executioner would push the first one through the heart for a speedy demise.

The Roman Arena

In ancient Rome, there were plenty of other ways to meet a public death. In one case, 4,500 prisoners were tied to stakes in groups of thirty at the Forum. The tendon at the back of the neck was cut and they were dragged out of the city while still half alive and left behind as carrion for vultures and dogs.

The arena was a popular method of executing condemned criminals, Christians, and other religious or political dissenters perceived to be the enemies of the State. The average untrained man stood no chance when pitted against a gladiator.

It was more common for crowds of condemned criminals to be herded naked into the arena. Armed only with rusty swords, they were forced to fight to the death. Attendants lashed them into action with whips and anyone who refused to fight risked having a red-hot branding iron pressed against his genitals. These wretched souls fought until only one man was left standing but there was no reprieve even for him. As he raised his arms in apparent victory, a black-helmeted giant carrying a two-handed axe would enter the arena and slice him in half.

Romans particularly enjoyed the re-enactment of mythological scenes. In a re-staging of *Pasiphae and the Bull,* in which the legendary queen of Crete conceived the Minotaur, a real bull was lowered in a cage and harnessed to a naked female victim. This act was presumably performed as an execution as it must surely have been fatal.

Christians were famously thrown to the lions. This punishment was originally added to the law books to deal with recalcitrant slaves, but other victims were found when it proved a popular entertainment. The most feared aggressor was the Libyan lion with its razor-sharp claws. Once captured, the beast would be sedated with copious quantities of Armenian brandy and shipped across the Mediterranean to the port of Ostia and up the river to Rome. There it would be caged and starved. Ravenous and fully sober, it would finally be released into the arena to face a crowd of defenceless victims who often had their feet fixed to hollow stones by molten lead. Some magicians claimed the power to halt a lion in its tracks with a series of hand gestures. One animal could be mesmerized – ten could not – so more than one lion was released.

Bulls, bears, and leopards were also used to kill victims. Criminals, known as *noxii,* were often exhibited on a platform in the middle of the arena and the creatures they were going to face were penned beneath. Saint Benignus of Dijon was torn apart by twelve half-starved dogs after hot needles were inserted under his fingernails. The slave girl Saint Blandina refused to renounce her faith and was tortured until her exhausted tormentors could think of nothing more to do to her. Blandina was taken to the arena again. Tied to a stake, she was not attacked by any of the wild animals set upon her, but she endured having to watch her fellow Christians perish for several days. After being scourged and placed on a hot grate, she was wrapped in a net and tossed around by wild bulls before finally being despatched with a dagger!

The demented Emperor Nero sometimes took on the part of the wild animal, dressing in animal skins and attacking men, women, and children tied naked to stakes. When Queen Boudicca of the Iceni tribe revolted, after her daughters had been raped and she herself had been stripped and flogged, Nero ordered further public punishments.

'Every kind of atrocity was inflicted upon their captives,' said the second-century historian Cassius Dio. 'They hung up the noblest and best-looking women naked, cutting off their breasts and stitching them to their mouths, so that the women appeared to be eating them and after this they impaled them on sharp stakes, run up the body.'

Left: Into the arena: Christians, or possibly gladiators, battle lions, armed only with a cloak and dagger.

Another punishment during Nero's reign was to force the prisoner to dig his own grave. A sharpened stake was then fixed to the bottom. The victim was bound hand and foot before being pushed into the pit. If his crime had been a minor one, he would be pushed so the stake pierced his heart and finished him off quickly. If he had been convicted of a more serious felony, the stake would pierce his groin and he would be left to die in agony or would perhaps be buried alive.

Being buried alive – after being scourged in public – was traditionally a punishment reserved for vestal virgins who had violated their chastity vows. The lucky ones were entombed in a small cave and left to starve. Nero inflicted this punishment on the priestess Rubria even though it was he who raped her.

Nero blamed the Christians for the burning of Rome in AD 64. He had them rounded up and ordered that they be 'lighted up, when the day declined, to serve as torches during the night'. They were tied to stakes, smeared with tar, and set alight to illuminate the gardens where the newly homeless sought refuge. However, this atrocity worked against him. Tacitus reported that the Christians behaved so bravely 'humanity relented in their favour'.

Defeated gladiators faced public execution if they were not killed in the arena outright but the emperor decided their ultimate fate. Usually the crowd bayed *'Jugula! Jugula!'* (Cut his throat! Cut his throat!) and most emperors sought to placate the spectators. If his thumb went down, the defeated gladiator would have to sit back on one heel, grip the winner's thigh, and tilt his head back. He would give a little nod to indicate that he was ready to die and his opponent would then quickly cut his throat as the dying man released his grip.

Some champions were real show-offs and took pride in spelling out the emperor's name in their victims' blood.

Caligula's Games

If a gladiatorial contest went on for too long during the reign of the bloodthirsty, and possibly insane, Emperor Caligula (AD 37-41), the Emperor would call a halt and order the two participants to cut each other's throats for a bit of instant action. At least two deaths an hour were required in the arena for prime entertainment if the audience was not to become bored.

Even the victor was not safe: protocol demanded that he take on the next contender. If he was one of the emperor's favourites, however, he could be excused and the emperor would then throw money into the crowds of spectators to assuage them.

If one of the combatants lost his nerve and refused to fight on, say, his first appearance in the arena, the crowd would hiss and cry, *'Hoc habet'* (He's had

it). At a nod from Caligula, his opponent would step aside and an Armenian dwarf in gold costume would enter the arena. Armed with a vast array of weapons, he would kill the disgraced gladiator in the most painful way possible. The dwarf's lethal skill was so awesome that the crowd fell silent as the victim's screams could be heard echoing around not just the arena but the surrounding hills. Within minutes, he would be chopped into pieces and the dwarf would desecrate his remains.

After each bout, the bald, black-clad 'carrion man' came into the arena carrying a red-hot poker and a silver hammer. He would apply the poker to the genitals of the fallen. If there was no reaction, he assumed they were dead and struck them on the head with the hammer to release their souls. Anyone who was still alive but too injured to continue was dragged down to the 'finishing-off room' under the stadium where a professional butcher would despatch him with a few strokes of his meat cleaver.

Under Caligula, people were condemned to death in the arena without their case even being heard. The aged and infirm were matched against tired beasts. A famous writer was burnt alive for writing a line that contained a *double entendre*. The manager of the gladiators was chained up and beaten for days for some unspecified offence and was only killed when Caligula could no longer stand the stench of the decomposing brain.

Parents were forced to watch the execution of their children. One man was brought on a litter when he pleaded that he was too ill to attend. Another was invited to dine with Caligula shortly after his son was executed for being too well-dressed and coiffed. The grieving man was asked to dinner once again on the day of the funeral and attended because he feared for the life of his other son. Caligula was also bald so anyone with a good head of hair risked, at the very least, having it shaved off.

Ptolemy was condemned to the arena for wearing a purple cloak that was much admired. Aesius Proculus, a particularly tall and handsome man, was dragged from his seat in the amphitheatre and forced to take on two gladiators. When he beat both opponents, Caligula ordered his death after displaying him to the ladies, bound and clad in rags.

Men of rank were branded on the face, shut up in cages like animals, or sawn in half. When the actor Apelles was asked the question: 'Who is greater, Jupiter, the king of the gods, or Caligula?', the madman had him cut to pieces with a whip because he hesitated before answering. As Apelles pleaded for mercy under torture, the emperor praised his voice and the melodious quality of his groans.

Caligula instructed his executioners to take their time and 'strike a man so that he feels he is dying'. He ordered one senator to be slit open and his eyes and internal organs removed with red-hot pincers (in that order) to prolong his agony. The man was then sawn in half and torn to pieces. Caligula's lust for cruelty, however, was not satisfied until he saw the man's limbs, bowels, and other body parts dragged through the street and piled up before him. He was so numb to the sight of pain and blood that he often ordered torture or decapitation as entertainment while he ate.

The Cruelties of Domitian

The Emperor Domitian (81–96) was particularly tough on Christians and, one way or another, a slow, painful, humiliating, and very public death was in store for them. They were hacked to pieces, burned to death, or perforated with a stake. Spikes, pincers, and iron claws would be used to tear the flesh from their bones and honey would be rubbed on their skin so insects would sting them to death.

The faithful would also be strung up by one leg, their thumbs, or their hair. Women's breasts would be cut off. Machinery would be used to crush victims or they would be beaten to death with hammers, whips, or cudgels.

Martyrs were smeared with honey and milk before being nailed into barrels and force-fed. Parasites would then feed on their internal organs as their bodies rotted from the outside. It could take two weeks to die.

Victims were also skinned alive or roasted. After being sewn inside an animal's carcass, they would be left to die in the sun unless the vultures got there first. Others were boiled in oil or had molten lead poured over them. Eyes were torn out, limbs severed, and genitals torn.

Saint Cyrilla's belly was slit open and filled with hot coals. Saint Euphemia was forced to watch her severed limbs being fried in a large pan. Roasting on a gridiron (a frame made of iron bars the thickness of a finger) was another unpleasant option. Three bars ran lengthways to the height of a man while

Below: The martyrdom of St Lawrence on a gridiron. The saint reputedly asked to be turned over when one side was 'cooked'

seven or eight shorter pieces ran crosswise, forming a grill. More bars braced the structure and there were short legs on each corner. A fire was lit underneath and the victim was pinioned with iron forks.

Numerous saints were broiled alive in public in this way, among them Saint Laurence, whose famous wit proved to be his downfall. When the Emperor Valerian (253–260) asked him to hand over the treasures of his church, he sent the widows and orphans in his care. Being sentenced to be martyred on the gridiron did not seem to quell his spirit in any way. After

Below: Inquisitors obtain confessions by the use of various instruments of torture, including the brazen bull in which the victim was placed and roasted alive

some time over the fire, he is reputed to have said, 'This side is roasted enough, oh great tyrant; you decide whether roasted or raw makes better meat.' When they turned him over, he said, 'Now it's done to a turn; you can start eating.' Pagan onlookers reported that he gave off a malodorous stench. Believers smelt a sweet odour and saw him bathed in heavenly light. Some Roman senators converted on the spot. As he died, Saint Laurence prayed that Rome would convert to Christianity. His body is buried on the Via Tiburtina.

The saint's death heralded the end of Roman paganism. When the Emperor Diocletian (284–305) was upbraided by his chamberlain for executing Christians on the gridiron, the unfortunate man was hung up and scourged. Vinegar and salt were rubbed into his wounds and he was sent to the gridiron and cooked over a slow fire. After that, any idolatry was forbidden and Laurence's prayer was answered. The basilica of San Lorenzo, begun by Constantine, Diocletian's successor, to commemorate the death of Laurence, stands to this day.

Another version of the gridiron was the metal chair on which the victim was forced to sit as it was heated from underneath. Seven women who had collected drops of Saint Blaise's blood, after he had been tortured with hot combs and beheaded in 316, were sentenced to die in this way. Seven brass chairs were sent for and the women were forced to sit on them. Fires were then lit until they were 'so hot that sparks flew from them as from a furnace heated to the utmost, and their bodies were so scorched that all the people that stood by were savored of the frying'.

Inside the Bull

In the sixth century BC, the Athenian artist Perillus invented the brass bull – a new and original instrument of torture. Brass was used because it heated up quickly. The person was forced into the hollow belly of the animal through a trapdoor in its backside. As an added refinement, Perillus placed flutes inside the nostrils of the beast so that the victim's cries would simulate the bellowing of a bull.

According to the first-century BC historian Diodorus of Sicily, Perillus showed his invention to Phalaris, the tyrant of Acragas (modern-day Agrigento in Sicily), a man famed for his cruelty, expecting a handsome reward. Phalaris was impressed, but before handing over any money, he asked Perillus to climb inside and imitate the cries of a dying man so he could test whether the device really worked. The inventor obeyed: the door was shut and the fire was lit under it.

When Phalaris was satisfied that Perillus' screams did indeed sound like the bellowing of a bull he had him pulled out while still alive, not wanting to spoil the bull. The hapless inventor was thrown from a cliff and his body denied a proper burial. Although in Diodorus' account Phalaris behaves in this way due to his outrage at the cruelty of Perillus, in other writers' accounts of the episode, the bull proves to be Phalaris' downfall. The people of Acragas found this method of public execution so cruel that they rebelled and deposed him. The tyrant had his tongue torn out before being slowly burned to death inside the bronze bull. Several Christian martyrs also perished in this way, among them Saints Eustachius, Pelagia, and Antipas. The latter perhaps died inside a bronze horse rather than a bull.

'The Butcher'

The arrogant and bloodthirsty Emperor Macrinus (217–218) crucified his own soldiers for minor offences and revelled in inflicting punishments on them that were reserved for slaves. Faced with mutiny, he decimated his troops by killing one in ten. For mere grumbling, he 'centimated' them – killing one in a hundred – claiming that this was merciful for troops who deserved to be decimated.

He was also a stickler when it came to sex. When he discovered that a number of his soldiers had had intercourse with the same female servant (even though she had a reputation for being promiscuous), he ordered two large oxen to be cut open and, without even asking the men whether the accusations were true, had them all sewn up inside, with their heads poking out so they could 'talk to each other' as they died! His biographer Julius Capitolinus commented, 'Thus did he inflict a penalty on them, although punishments like this were not decreed even for adulteries by our ancestors or in these days'.

While the Romans were out fighting the Parthians in modern-day Iran, a tribune failed to organize the watch properly. He was tied up and dragged under a wheeled carriage, alive at first, then dead. Floggings were frequent. Macrinus also re-introduced an ancient punishment that had been popular with the Etruscan tyrant Mezentius. It involved tying a person to a corpse and leaving them to die 'consumed by slow putrefaction'.

Runaway slaves were sentenced to swordfights in the Roman arena where they were certain to die at the hands of skilled gladiators. Victims were immured; informers who did not prove their case were executed; the few who did were first given money then sent away in disgrace. The worst punishment was reserved for those caught in adulterous acts. The couple would be bound together before being burned to death. Macrinus was so sadistic that his own slaves called him *Macellinus* (the butcher) because the walls of his house were drenched with the blood of his slaves and it looked like a slaughterhouse. With a track record such as this, it perhaps comes as no great surprise to learn that he was killed in a rebellion after only fourteen months in power.

Roman Inventiveness

There were other unsavoury ways to die in public in ancient Rome. Those found guilty of bigamy or patricide were wrapped in lead sheets or tied in sacks and thrown into the River Tiber. The Greeks and the Romans also executed prisoners by throwing them from the tops of temples and steep hills. Every bone in the body would be broken as victims came crashing down the sides of buildings or the mountainsides. If they survived at all, they were left to die of shock or exposure to the elements. The luckier ones died of heart failure or on impact.

It was believed that Aesop, author of the famous *Fables*, was flung from a cliff in the year 561 BC after stealing treasures from the temple of Apollo. In Rome, murderers and traitors were thrown from the Tarpeian Rock, a method of execution that was revived in sixteenth-century France.

The Romans also invented a cruel method for breaking a victim's body: a heavy iron-rimmed wheel that was propelled forward by an executioner carrying a hammer. Every bone was broken along the way. In some versions, the victim was strapped to the ground or faced outwards from the rim of the wheel. If the face was strapped, it was crushed by the hammer-wielding executioner. A fire might be lit under the wheel to add discomfort.

The Jewish historian Josephus saw two Christians martyred in this way. 'The executioners were ordered to bring the Christian prisoner in,' he wrote. 'His tunic was torn off and he was bound hand and foot with thongs, and fixed to the great wheel. All his joints were dislocated and all his limbs smashed. The wheel was stained with blood and the burning coals in the grate beneath it were extinguished by the blood pouring into it. Lumps of flesh clumped around the axle and everywhere there were bits of flesh and bone. Another was fastened to the wheel and stretched and burned with fire. Sharp spits, heated until they were red-hot, were applied to his back and stuck in his sides and inwards, burning him dreadfully.'

If the wheel was smaller, the victim would be spread eagled across it. The wrists and ankles would be smashed so the hands and feet draped around the rim. Victims were also tied around the circumference of a wide and heavy wheel before being pushed down a hill, over a cliff, or simply around the city square until their bones and ribcage were beyond repair.

Another version involved putting a prisoner inside a barrel (lined with nails and spikes) that was then rolled down a hill. Captured during the First Punic War (264–241 BC), the Roman general Marcus Atilius Regulus was sent back to Rome to negotiate an exchange of prisoners. When this mission failed, he honourably returned to Carthage where he was tortured and rolled down a hill in a barrel full of spikes.

Saint Catherine of Alexandria was famously sentenced to be broken on the wheel, but she did not die on it, despite the firework named after her. In the fourth century, a new version of the wheel had just been developed: it had

Left: Thrown from the
Tarpeian Rock, a
surprisingly merciful end
for those found guilty of
treason in Rome

spikes around the rim and would also have been rolled over another row of
spikes that poked out of the ground. In the case of Catherine of Alexandria,
it did not prove successful. She lived during a time of intense Christian
persecution at the hands of the Emperor Maxentius (306–312), whom she
went to rebuke for his tyranny. She was barely eighteen and very beautiful.
Instead of putting her to death immediately, he summoned fifty philosophers
to argue with her but she emerged from the debate victorious. Several of her
adversaries converted and were put to death. Maxentius then tried to seduce
her but the virgin refused him and he had her scourged and imprisoned.

While Maxentius went off to inspect his military camp, his wife, fascinated
by the girl's courage and intransigence, went to visit her. When he returned,
he found that the empress and 200 soldiers had been converted. They were
killed – history is silent as to how – and Catherine herself was sentenced to
death on the spiked wheel. When she was put on it, her bonds miraculously
loosened and the wheel broke, its spikes shearing off, injuring many
onlookers. Maxentius then sentenced her to be beheaded : when Catherine's
head was severed, it is said a white, milky substance flowed from her veins.

Two Persian Monks

In antiquity, it was not just the Romans who publicly executed Christians. In 327, the eighteenth year of his reign, King Shapur the Great of Persia began a brutal persecution. This was more than likely spurred on by the knowledge that Constantine, the first Christian emperor of Rome, had declared himself the spiritual leader of all Christians, no matter where in the world they were from. This division of loyalty of his subjects Shapur could not tolerate, and set to work making sure that he himself would be uppermost in the minds of his citizens. Churches and monasteries were destroyed: any Christians who agreed to make sacrifices to the pagan gods were spared, but those who refused were tortured and killed. Constantine wrote to the Persian king entreating him to stop the persecution but to no avail.

Hearing that nine Christians had been imprisoned under sentence of death, two monks named Jonas and Barachisius turned up at the jail and declared that they also were ready to die for their faith. Once the other nine were dead, Jonas and Barachisius were asked to make a sacrifice to the sun, water, or fire. They refused and were brought before the chief justice who had condemned the other victims. The judges urged the two priests to obey the King of Kings – Shapur – and worship the elements but they replied it was more sensible to obey a God in Heaven than a king on earth.

Jonas was forced to lay down with a sharp stake under his midriff and was beaten with whips and rods. He would not yield and sustained himself by praying so the judges ordered that he spend the night in a frozen pond. Barachisius was examined next. When he once again refused to conduct a pagan sacrifice, he was scalded with hot pitch and sent back to jail to spend the night suspended from one foot.

The following morning, Jonas was brought back from the pond and asked whether he had had an uncomfortable night. 'No,' he said. 'From the day I came into this world, I never remember a more peaceful night for I was wonderfully refreshed by the memory of the sufferings of Christ.' He was then told that his companion had renounced. 'I know,' said Jonas, 'He renounced the Devil and his angels long ago.' The judges asked whether it was not better for him to give up his God and save himself. 'Corn that is saved does not multiply,' replied Jonas, 'Our life is seed, sown to rise again in the world to come.'

The judges then cut off his fingers and toes, telling him he could have them back at harvest time. Jonas was thrown into a vat of hot pitch and afterwards crushed in a wooden press. His body was finally cut up with a saw and the pieces flushed down a sewer, with guards in attendance in case any Christians tried to grab the pieces as relics. Barachisius was then told that the same fate awaited him if he still refused to make a sacrifice. When he still would not , the judges ordered him impaled on a stake, after which his bones were crushed in a press, and boiling pitch was poured down his throat.

CHAPTER 2

Beheading

From the beginning of civilization, beheading was widely used as a form of capital punishment. The axe was wielded in ancient Assyria and Egypt: a famous relief in the British Museum shows the mass decapitation of Chaldean prisoners after their defeat by the Assyrians. Decapitation was also the prescribed mode of execution in ancient China.

The Victorian hangman James Berry, who wrote *My Experiences As An Executioner*, was particularly impressed with the Chinese methods. 'In China, decapitation has been reduced almost to a science,' he said, 'and the Chinese executioners are probably the most skilful headsmen in the world. I have in my possession a Chinese executioner's knife with which the heads of nine pirates were severed in nine successive blows and a terrible knife it is and well-fitted for the purpose.'

The Greek historian Xenophon declared that beheading was the most honourable form of death in the fourth century BC. Decapitation by sword was thought to be less degrading than by the axe.

The Romans also beheaded prisoners. Although beheading (*decollatio* or *capitis amputato*) was normally reserved as a military punishment, Caligula kept a skilled headsman ready to decapitate those prisoners he chose at random from his jails. A block called a *cippus* (Latin for 'tombstone') was placed in front of a dug pit so the head could fall into it. The victim was first tied to a stake and scourged, then dragged to the block, held down, and beheaded. This was originally done by axe but a sword was later used on Roman citizens. Like the Greeks, they considered it a more honourable instrument of execution.

If the victim was lucky, the head was removed in a single stroke. Saint

Below: Traditional Chinese execution by beheading with a sword. The Chinese executioners were skilled, and took pride in beheading their victims with a single blow

Cecilia was not so fortunate but then she was inured to suffering. She famously wore a coarse garment under her gown to mortify her flesh. Although she had pledged her virginity to Christ, her father had other ideas and married her off to a patrician named Valerian. Her husband only heard of her Christian vows on their wedding night when she proceeded to convert him and he, in turn, converted his brother. Both were martyred, along with a man who had become a Christian after witnessing their fortitude. All three were beheaded by sword out of respect for their rank. Saint Cecilia was sentenced to be suffocated in her own bathhouse and the furnace was fed with seven times the normal amount of fuel, but still she survived. A soldier was sent to despatch her but three blows of the sword (the maximum number permitted by law) failed to separate her head from her body. She survived for three more days with Christians flocking to her house to witness what they took to be a miracle.

Beheading in England

The tradition of an honourable death by beheading was continued in England, though scourging before decapitation was omitted. Hanging was usually reserved for the lower classes. Rebellious noblemen who had been sentenced to be hanged, drawn, and quartered for treason were understandably relieved when their sentence was changed to beheading. Many a peer of the realm went to the scaffold with a good grace, knowing that they could make a parting speech before departing this life in a relatively swift and painless manner.

Although there may well have been beheadings in England before then, the introduction of decapitation as a form of punishment is attributed to William the Conqueror. The first person to fall foul of it was Waltheof, Earl of Northumbria, an ancestor of the Scottish kings through the marriage of his daughter to David I. He submitted to William the Conqueror in 1066 but joined the rebels in the north in 1069. When the rebellion failed, he was returned to favour by his marriage to Judith, William's niece, but was implicated in a second revolt in 1075, tried for treason, and condemned. Why he was sentenced to death is not clear. Those who had fought against William at the Battle of Hastings were simply stripped of their lands and Morcar, Earl of Northumbria, who had rebelled in 1071, was imprisoned for life. Only Waltheof paid with his head and he was imprisoned in Winchester for almost a year before the sentence was carried out. The earl was said to have spent his last days as a penitent praying and fasting while Archbishop Lanfranc continued to argue his innocence. On 31 May 1076, Waltheof was hurried to St Giles's Hill, outside the city. After donating his clothes to the poor, he knelt at the block and began reciting the Lord's Prayer. Perhaps feeling that this was all taking too long, the executioner drew his sword and struck Waltheof as he uttered the words, 'Lead us not into temptation...' According to witnesses, Waltheof's severed head completed the line in a clear voice. His body was then flung into a ditch.

Both the English and the Normans at court were horrified by William's treatment of Waltheof. He had obviously lost patience with rebellious Englishmen and Waltheof's death put an end to further insurrections. Traitors traditionally forfeited their property to the Crown but Judith was allowed to keep the earldom of Huntingdon; perhaps because she had given evidence of her husband's guilt or maybe just because she was William's niece. A fortnight after the execution, Abbot Wulfketel of Crowland retrieved Waltheof's body and, at his widow's request, gave it an honourable burial in the chapterhouse of his monastery.

The Axe

The axe was soon after introduced to English beheadings. This was not the standard axe used for chopping wood but a special 'heading axe'. From the haft, the blade broadened out towards a cutting edge that was curved. The blade was around sixteen inches from haft to edge and the cutting edge measured ten inches in length.

The heading axe on display at the Tower of London is poorly balanced and roughly made. It weighs nearly eight pounds and the shaft is three feet long. The blade itself is black and rough, looking as if it had come direct from the blacksmith's forge. Neither sharp nor polished, this fearsome tool was deliberately designed as a deterrent for it simply shattered its way through the spinal column rather than cutting it in two. Although there was once a fearsome array of 'heading axes' in the Tower of London, the one now kept in the Bowyer Tower is thought to be the one that removed Lord Lovat's head in 1747. He was the last Englishman to be beheaded.

Usually made of oak, the block was originally just a piece of tree trunk about two feet high so the victim could rest his neck on it in a dignified, kneeling position. A shorter block was sometimes used to deliberately humiliate the victim. The block on which Charles I was executed at Whitehall on 30 January 1649 was just ten inches tall, which forced him to lie down for his execution. It was rectangular with the top scalloped out on both sides. One side had a wider hollow to accommodate the prisoner's shoulders; the other side was smaller for the head. The narrow isthmus in between supported the front of the neck to steady it from the blow received to the back. The blocks were usually custom-made for each execution or series of executions and, again, the one in the Bowyer Tower is thought to have been made specifically for Lord Lovat.

If the head came off with a single blow, beheading was probably the most humane form of capital punishment. Severing the brain from the spinal cord ensured an immediate death; within seconds, the victim also suffered severe

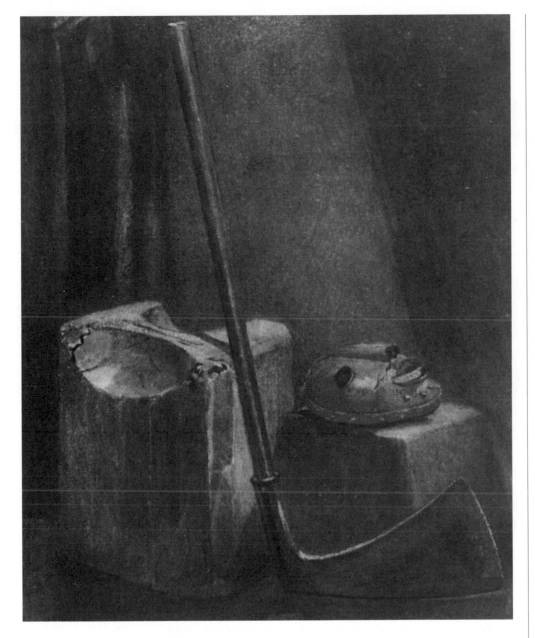

Left: The block, axe and executioner's mask once used at the Tower of London, and still on display there

shock and a fatal loss of blood pressure. Was it painful? It has been reported that the eyes and mouths of people executed in this way still showed signs of movement after beheading. It has also been estimated that there is enough oxygen left in the brain for a decapitated head to function for a few seconds more. This is the moment when the victim is most likely to feel acute pain. However, he or she could lose consciousness within seconds once the supply of blood to the brain has been cut off.

Beheading on Tower Hill

Between 1388 and 1747, ninety-one people were publicly beheaded outside the walls of the Tower of London on Tower Hill (a permanent scaffold stood there in the fifteenth and sixteenth centuries). Only eight beheadings

Above: Lady Jane Grey, the 'Nine-Days Queen', is beheaded on Tower Hill, 12 February 1554

actually took place inside the Tower. All were well-attended as the victims were prominent people: Lord Hastings who was executed during the Wars of the Roses; two of Henry VIII's wives, Anne Boleyn and Catherine Howard, along with Lady Rochford, a lady-in-waiting; a supporter of Catherine of Aragon, Margaret Pole, Countess of Salisbury; fifteen-year-old Lady Jane Grey who was queen of England for just nine days in 1553; her husband, Lord Guildford Dudley; and Robert Devereux, the second Earl of Essex, who tried to persuade the people of London to revolt in 1601.

While it is likely that Anne Boleyn was innocent of the charges levelled against her, there is little doubt that 22-year-old Catherine Howard committed adultery, an indiscretion that constituted treason for the wife of a monarch. She admitted to an affair with Thomas Culpepper, amongst other lovers. Unlike Anne, Catherine was not given the option of being decapitated by sword but faced the axe instead. Unsure that she could keep her composure in the face of this punishment, she asked that the block and the executioner be brought to her room the night before her death. She knelt down in his presence and 'laid her head in that horrible hollow'. As she rose to her feet, she declared herself prepared to go through the ordeal with grace and propriety – which she did. Once on the scaffold, Catherine told the onlookers, 'I die a queen but would rather die the wife of Culpepper'. Despatched by one stroke of the axe, she had been married to the king for just one year, six months, and four days. Culpepper was already dead. At his trial in Guildhall on 1 December 1541, he said: 'Gentlemen, do not seek to know more than that the king deprived me of the thing I love best in the world and, though you may hang me for it, she loves me as well as I love her.' Having condemned himself with his own words, he was found guilty of treason along with Francis Dereham, who had had an earlier affair with Catherine. However, the statutory sentence of hanging, drawing, and quartering was commuted to beheading. Both were executed at Tyburn on 10 December 1541.

The elderly Margaret Pole, Countess of Salisbury, had been caught up in the machinations surrounding Henry VIII and faced execution in the Tower. After being imprisoned for two years without trial, she was finally led on to the scaffold. When ordered to put her head on the block, she refused and said, 'So should traitors do, and I am none'. The executioner insisted but the redoubtable countess shook her head and, according to an eyewitness, told him, 'if he would have her head, to get it off best he could; so that he was constrained to fetch it off slovenly'. He chased her around the block, lunging at her with his axe until she fell, mutilated and dead. Margaret's body was buried at the Chapel Royal of Saint Peter and Vincula within the precincts of the Tower.

Lady Jane Grey insisted on blindfolding herself but then could not find the block. 'What shall I do? Where is it?' she said. A bystander guided her to it. She laid her head on the block and announced: 'Lord into thy hands I commend my spirit.' The axe came down.

Sir Thomas More had fallen foul of Henry VIII nearly twenty years earlier and was beheaded on 6 July 1535. Having put on his finest silk gown for the occasion, he was advised by the Lieutenant of the Tower to wear something less magnificent as the executioner always kept the dead man's clothes and his expensive apparel should rightfully remain in his family. More carried a painted red cross up to Tower Hill and, when he mounted the scaffold, the executioner knelt down and begged his forgiveness. More kissed the man and said: 'I forgive thee. Pluck up thy spirits, man, and be not afraid to do thy office. I am sorry my neck is short, therefore strike not awry.' He put his head on the block and the executioner was just about to swing the axe when More signalled for a moment's delay. 'I pray you let me lay my beard over the block lest ye should cut it,' he said. 'Pity that should be cut that has not committed treason.' Once his beard was moved, the axe fell and he was despatched with a single stroke. Some were not so lucky. Sir Thomas More was canonized in 1935.

How a Queen Dies

Mary Queen of Scots was held prisoner by Elizabeth I, Henry VIII's daughter, for eighteen years before being sent to the block on 8 February 1587. A scaffold was built in the Great Hall at Fotheringhay Castle, her place of captivity near Peterborough in Northamptonshire. When the executioner asked for her forgiveness, she said, 'I forgive you with all my heart, for now I hope you shall make an end of all my troubles.' The executioner and two ladies-in-waiting helped her take off her gown. Mary was rather indignant about undressing in front of so many people and complained that 'she had never seen so many grooms to make her unready, and that she had never put off her clothes in such company'. Nevertheless, it was noted that she prepared herself quickly as if eager to leave this life and did not cry.

She was blindfolded with a white cloth embroidered in gold that also served to tie her hair up, leaving her neck exposed. Her two ladies-in-waiting left the scaffold and Mary knelt on a cushion in front of the block. Stretching out her arms, she said: *'In manus tuas, Domine, commendo spiritum meum'* (Into your hands, O Lord, I commend my spirit) three or four times. The executioner's assistant put a hand on her body to steady it. Even so, the first swing of the axe missed her neck completely and struck her on the back of the head. The queen's lips moved and her servants said they heard her utter 'sweet Jesus'. With any luck, the blow merely stunned her. The second stroke was on target but failed to sever her head and the executioner had no choice but to saw it off. Finally, he raised the severed head and cried, 'God save the Queen!'. He meant Elizabeth I.

It was reported that Mary's lips continued moving for fifteen minutes after she had been executed. Her little dog also reportedly hid up her skirts and had to be forcibly pulled out before it lay down between her head and shoulders. Covered with blood, it was taken away to be washed.

Mary's head was displayed from a bay window so that crowds of people could see that the Scottish queen was dead. It was reunited with her body, embalmed, and buried at Peterborough on 1 August 1587. The gravedigger was said to be 'Old Scarlett', the same man who had dug the grave of Catherine of Aragon. When Mary's son, James I, came to the throne of England, he had her body dug up and reburied at Westminster Abbey. Fotheringhay Castle was knocked down.

Death of an English Hero

Sir Walter Raleigh, the celebrated sailor, explorer, and scholar, was a favourite of Elizabeth I but fell foul of James I of England (VI of Scotland) who locked him away in the Tower for thirteen years. He eventually persuaded the monarch to let him lead an expedition to find El Dorado, the legendary city of gold up the Orinoco River in Guyana, on condition he did not offend Spain with whom James was seeking an alliance. Raleigh failed to find gold and set fire to a Spanish settlement so, on his return to England, he was sent to the scaffold in Old Palace Yard, Westminster, on 29 October 1618 (the day of the Lord Mayor's Parade). Still popular with the public, it was hoped the 'pageants and fine shewes might draw away the people from beholding the tragedie of one of the gallantest worthies that ever England bred'. It failed. When one of his friends complained that he could not get near the scaffold because so many people had come to see the execution, Raleigh said to him: 'I know not what shift you will make – but I am sure to have a place'. He faced his ordeal with typical *sang froid*. When his jailer brought him a cup of the new sack wine brought over from Spain that morning, and asked him whether he enjoyed it, Raleigh said, 'It was a fine drink if you could tarry over it'.

Sir Walter had always been a flashy dresser with pearls in his ears and on his shoes, diamonds on the fingers of both hands, and rubies and emeralds embroidered on his clothes. For his execution he wore a sombre black cap and velvet gown with ash-grey silk stockings. He usually wore his hair in the latest Italian fashion but, that morning, he turned his barber away saying, 'Let them comb it, that shall have it'.

Raleigh had recently suffered a stroke that caused him to drag his left leg. On the day of his execution, he limped to the scaffold and even this appeared heroic as it was the same leg he had injured when fighting the Spanish. Raleigh made a long and moving speech, forgiving his enemies and refuting all the charges brought against him. He asked for divine forgiveness, admitting that he was 'a man full of vanity' and that he had lived 'a sinful life, in all sinful callings, having been a soldier, a captain, a sea captain, and a courtier, which are all places of wickedness and vice'. He then turned to the kneeling, hooded axeman, put his hands on the man's shoulders, forgave him, and unexpectedly said: 'Show me thine axe'. The executioner was

Right: Sir Walter Raleigh meets his end with typical composure, remarking to the executioner that his axe was 'a sharp medicine...a physician for all my disease'

confused: he did not think it proper to show a man the weapon that was going to kill him but Raleigh asked again. The executioner held out the axe. Raleigh ran his finger down the blade and said, 'This blade give me no fear. It is a sharp medicine…a physician for all my diseases'.

Echoing the story that Sir Walter Raleigh had spread his cloak over a puddle to keep Elizabeth I's feet dry, the executioner now spread his cloak on the scaffold for the nobleman to kneel on. The executioner asked the condemned whether he wished to face the east and Raleigh answered: 'If the heart be straight, it is no matter which way the head lieth'. He knelt, briefly prayed, and said to the executioner, 'When I stretch forth my hands, despatch me', but when he did, the headsman hesitated. 'What dost thou fear?' said Raleigh. 'Strike man, strike.' The executioner did so – twice. Even so, it was noticed that the body never moved or twitched though the lips continued to move in prayer.

The head was shown from both sides of the scaffold and put in a red leather bag. It was later given to Lady Raleigh who kept it with her until she died twenty-nine years later. Her son, Carew, then took it and was said to be buried with it. Sir Walter's body was buried at St Margaret's in Westminster.

To Kill a King

The most momentous beheading in British history was the execution of Charles I at Whitehall on 30 January 1649. After losing the English Civil War, he was tried by a parliamentary court and found guilty of treason for having declared war on his people. A scaffold was built outside the Banqueting Hall so thousands could witness his death. The execution should have taken place early in the morning, but was delayed until an ordinance could be rushed through Parliament at the last minute, declaring it treason for anyone to be proclaimed as the dead king's successor. Charles did not appear on the scaffold until two o'clock that afternoon, famously wearing two shirts so he would not be seen shivering in the winter cold and so give the impression that he was afraid.

People thronged the streets, leaned through windows, and perched on roofs and chimneys for a good view. From the scaffold, Charles proclaimed himself a 'martyr for the people'. Some of the spectators agreed with him while others came to celebrate the death of a tyrant. 'There is but one stage more,' said William Juxon, Archbishop of Canterbury, 'which, though turbulent and troublesome, yet is very short…It will carry you from earth to heaven… to a crown of glory.' Charles gave Juxon a gold £5 or £6 piece bearing the head that he was about to lose and presented his jailer, Sir Thomas Herbert, with his silver alarm watch. This was a private joke between the two men: Charles had complained that Herbert needed an alarm clock so he could rise early enough to wake the king and had one ordered from a

London watchmaker. At the time of the beheading, it had not yet arrived.

There were two black-clad figures on the scaffold. One was seemingly old and was thought to be Richard Brandon, the public executioner. It was rumoured he was a reluctant regicide, and had to be 'fetched from his bed by a troop of horses and escorted to the scaffold site'. The other was a young, fair-haired man thought to be William Lowen, a former dunghill cleaner. They wore masks, false beards, and thick coats to prevent anyone from recognizing them. If the monarchy was restored, they would have been guaranteed a terrible death.

Charles handed his cloak and his Order of the Garter to Juxon. While he was having a word with the archbishop, he noticed someone trying to touch the axe. Afraid that this person might blunt the edge and cause a repetition of the agonizing death of his grandmother, Mary Queen of Scots, he pleaded, 'Hurt not the axe, that it may not hurt me'. He complained that the block was too low, making him lie face down in a humiliating position. 'It might be a little higher,' he said. 'It can be no higher,' the executioner replied.

The reason the block was so low was that fixings had been made to the boards around it in case the king refused to submit and had to be tied down. They need not have worried. Like all those with breeding, who were allowed a beheading instead of a more gruesome death, Charles knew how to die with dignity and no restraints were necessary. He asked his executioner to deliver the blow when he gave a sign by stretching out his arms. 'Yes, I will, as it please your Majesty,' said the executioner. 'Does my hair bother you?' asked Charles, tucking it under a white satin cap. He urged the executioner to do his work and not put him in any pain. The man agreed.

Charles lay down and started to pray. Realizing that the executioner was now standing in position above him, he declared, 'Wait for the sign – wait for the sign'. According to one eyewitness, he stretched his arms out after some time and the executioner brought down the axe: 'Then suddenly with one blow, his head sped from his shoulders, and a universal groan, the like never heard before, broke from the dense and countless multitude'. The executioner's assistant held up the head: 'Behold the head of a traitor'. Britain was a republic.

A week later, Charles I was buried at Windsor. The republic was short-lived. In 1660, following the death of Oliver Cromwell, Lord Protector of England for the duration of the English Republic, Charles's son returned to the throne as Charles II. Although the executioners were never identified, the remaining regicides – those who had signed the death warrant – were rounded up and executed. No mercy of the axe for them: they were hanged, drawn, and quartered. The three men who had already died, including tOliver Cromwell and John Bradshaw, president of the court that had condemned Charles I, were dug up and hanged at Tyburn. The bodies were then nailed to London Bridge, where they were left to decay.

Facing page: The execution of King Charles I, a momentous event in English history that would see the nation governed as a republic for a decade

Jack Ketch the Bungler

Charles I's grandson, the Duke of Monmouth, had an even worse time of it than his great-great-grandmother Mary Queen of Scots. The illegitimate son of Charles II, Monmouth proclaimed himself king after the death of his father but his rebellion was crushed by James II, Charles's brother, the legitimate heir to the throne. Monmouth went to the scaffold on Tower Hill on 15 July 1685 and was unlucky enough to get as executioner one Jack Ketch, a man so notorious for his barbarous incompetence that for the next two centuries the nickname 'Jack Ketch' was given to all England's hangmen.

'Here are six guineas for you,' said Monmouth, handing over the coins (about £800 in today's money). 'Pray do your business well. Do not hack me as you did Lord Russell. I have heard you struck him three or four times.' Russell had in fact been struck only twice although a knife had been used to finish off the job. 'If you strike me twice, I cannot promise not to move,' he continued. 'My servant will give you some more gold if you do the work well.' He took off his wig and coat, refused to be blindfolded, and knelt down with his neck on the block before raising himself back up again. 'Prithee, let me feel the axe,' he said. Ketch proffered it and Monmouth felt the edge. 'I fear it is not sharp enough,' he said. 'It is sharp and heavy enough,' said Ketch.

This exchange did little for the executioner's composure. His first swing inflicted only a flesh wound. Monmouth got to his feet and looked reproachfully at him before kneeling back down. After two more strokes, the head had not been severed and the body was still moving. After the third stroke, Ketch threw down the axe and said, 'I cannot do it; my heart fails me'. He offered forty guineas (over £5,000 today) to anyone who would finish the job for him. 'Take up the axe, man,' the sheriff told Ketch. 'Fling him over the rails!' cried the mob, swearing to kill Ketch if he did not finish off the job.

After another couple of blows, Monmouth had stopped moving and Ketch finished the job with a knife. It had taken at least five strokes and maybe more than eight to despatch Monmouth. By this time, the mob was in a frenzy. They dipped their handkerchiefs in the blood, because many of them considered Monmouth a martyr of the Protestant faith. Ketch was in danger of being torn to pieces by the crowd and had to be escorted away.

Monmouth's remains were taken to the Chapel Royal in the Tower of London, where he was to be buried. However, his head was sewn back on first so that, as son of the former king, he could sit for a royal portrait. The following year, Ketch was hanged for killing a woman. John Price, his executioner, later died on the same gallows.

Jacobite Rebels

Another unlucky victim was Arthur Elphinstone, Lord Balmerino. Captured after the Jacobite rising of 1746, he was put down at the Battle of Culloden.

Facing page: 31 May 1718: English executioner Jack Ketch, notorious for his incompetent or sadistic execution technique, is himself taken to be hanged for the murder of Elizabeth White

With fellow Jacobites, the lords Kilmarnock and Lovat, he was brought to London where they were tried, found guilty of treason, and sentenced to be hanged, drawn, and quartered. Although they refused to ask for clemency due to their aristocratic status, the sentence was commuted to beheading.

Balmerino and Kilmarnock were to go to the scaffold first. The warrant of execution was announced by the Deputy Lieutenant of the Tower, Lieutenant-General Adam Williamson, over dinner. Lady Balmerino promptly fainted. 'Lieutenant,' barked Balmerino. 'With your damned warrant you have spoiled my lady's stomach!'

On 18 August 1746, the two lords were allowed a farewell breakfast with their family and friends. They tossed a coin to see who got to go first. Kilmarnock won. Guarded by yeoman warders and soldiers with fixed bayonets, and followed by two hearses, Kilmarnock and Balmerino walked the short distance to the scaffold on Tower Hill. The prisoners had requested a block two feet high with a post underneath the scaffold to absorb the impact. Williamson noted that 'a piece of red Bais was supplied in which to catch their heads and not let them fall into the sawdust and filth of the stage'.

Balmerino and Kilmarnock were admirably calm and composed. Unfortunately, John Thrift, the executioner, was not. He was a perfectly adequate hangman but beheading had become a rare event. Bizarrely enough, he wore white for the occasion.

The execution of the Jacobites drew a huge crowd which assembled before dawn. They filled balconies, scaled roofs, and clung to the masts and the rigging of ships in the Pool of London. As the prisoners approached the scaffold, a huge roar went up. It was all too much for Thrift and he fainted. The officials on the scaffold revived him with a glass of wine.

Kilmarnock went first. When he mounted the scaffold, Thrift burst into tears. He gulped down more wine to steady his nerves. The earl stiffened him further by slipping a bag of money into his hand. After forgiving Thrift, Kilmarnock knelt down. Thrift advised him to remove his hands from the block 'lest they should be mangled or intercept the blow' then he stepped back, raised the axe, and waited for his lordship's signal. Dropping his handkerchief,

'the earl of Kilmarnock had his head severed from the body at one stroke, all but a little skin which with a little chop was soon separated. He had ordered one of his warders to attend as his valet de chambre, and to keep down his body from struggle or any violent convulsive motion, but it was observed by those on the scaffold that the body, on the stroke, sprung backwards from the block and lay flat on its back, dead and extended, with its head fastened by that little hold which the executioner chopped off. So that it is probable that whenever the head is severed from the body at one stroke, it will always give that convulsive spring or bounce.'

Kilmarnock had thoughtfully provided a little extra cash for fresh sawdust to be spread on the scaffold after his death so that Balmerino would not have to wade through the blood. However, Thrift's first swing, or Kilmarnock's bounce, had shifted the block and this would have unfortunate consequences for the second man.

Thrift took a moment to change into a new white suit before Balmerino climbed onto the scaffold. Defiant to the last, he wore a blue coat with red facings – the uniform of Bonnie Prince Charlie's rebel army – along with a tartan hat to signify his allegiance to Scotland. This had to be worn under his wig as tartan had been banned after Culloden. He also wore a woollen undershirt which he said would serve as his shroud.

In his speech from the scaffold, Balmerino calmly asked his friends to drink him 'ain degrae to heaven'. Addressing the crowds, he said that he had

Below: Lords Balmerino and Kilmarnock are executed by John Thrift on Tower Hill, August 1746. Proceedings did not go well for Lord Balmerino

been brought up in 'true, loyal and anti-revolution principles'. The revolution he was referring to was the Act of Union between England and Scotland and the replacement of the Stuarts with the Hanoverian line. He called Bonnie Prince Charlie, the grandson of James II, a man of 'incomparable sweetness…affability…compassion…justice…temperance… patience…courage'. In Balmerino's eyes, this man was the legitimate king of Great Britain.

Thrift asked Balmerino for forgiveness and he replied, 'Friend, you need not ask me to forgive you.' He gave Thrift three guineas (£3.15 or £400 in today's money) saying: 'I have never had much money, and this is all I have. I wish it were more, for your sake. I am sorry I can add nothing else but my coat and waistcoat', which he proceeded to take off and lay out on the scaffold. None of this helped to settle Thrift's nerves.

Balmerino took a moment to decide which side of the block he should kneel on. Then, according to a contemporary report in the Newgate Calendar, 'immediately, without trembling or changing his countenance, he knelt at the block, and having his arms stretched out, said: 'Oh Lord, reward my friends, forgive my enemies, and receive my soul', he gave the signal by letting his arms falls…' Balmerino's signal caught Thrift off balance '…but his uncommon firmness and intrepidity, and the unexpected suddenness of the signal so surprised the executioner, that although he struck the part directed, the blow was not given with strength enough to wound him very deep. Upon which it seemed as if he made an effort to turn his head towards the executioner, and the under-jaw fell and returned very quickly, like anger and gnashing the teeth…A second blow immediately succeeding the first rendered him quite insensible, and a third finished the work.'

Thrift fared little better on 8 December, when he beheaded Charles Radcliffe, younger brother of the earl of Derwentwater, who was himself executed after the 1715 uprising. Radcliffe escaped from Newgate Prison while under sentence of death, but had been recaptured on a French ship taking arms back to Scotland for the 1745 uprising. He gave Thrift ten guineas (£10.50 or over £1,300 in today's money). Again, the executioner took three strokes to remove the unfortunate man's head.

The Last English Beheading

Finally, Lord Lovat, another supporter of the Jacobite '45 Rising, had asked to be beheaded in Edinburgh by an early guillotine called the Scottish Maiden. It was described in the *Complete Newgate Calendar* as being

'in the form of a painter's easel and about ten feet high; at four from the bottom is a cross-bar, on which the felon lays his head, which is kept down by another placed above. In the inner edges of the frame are grooves; in these is placed a sharp axe,

with a vast weight of lead, supported at the very summit by a peg; to that peg is fastened a cord, which the executioner cutting, makes the axe fall, and does the affair effectually, without suffering the unhappy criminal to undergo a repetition of strokes, as has been the case in the common method.'

The design of the Scottish Maiden was based on that of the Halifax Gibbet, a machine where the cord attached to the peg holding up the axe was pulled by every man who was present, unless the victim had been condemned for stealing livestock. In that case, the cord was tied to the stolen animal, whereupon the beast was whipped. As it pulled away, it also pulled out the peg and effectively became the executioner. The earl of Morton saw this procedure in full swing and was so impressed that he built a similar contraption – which became known as the Scottish Maiden – in Edinburgh in 1565. It despatched some 120 prisoners, including the earl of Morton himself.

The Maiden was so reliable that it was little wonder Lovat would have preferred it to the tender mercies of John Thrift. The king, however, refused his request: Lovat would face the axe just as his fellow rebels had done.

On 9 April 1747, Lovat rose at five in the morning, took a couple of glasses of wine and water, and combed out his wig. He then breakfasted on minced veal, washed down with more wine and water. Asked by a major in the Tower how he felt about his forthcoming demise, he replied: 'Why, I am about doing very well, for I am preparing myself, sir, for a place where hardly any majors, and very few Lieutenant-Generals go'. It was mid-morning when the Sheriff escorted him to Tower Hill, where a huge crowd had been gathering since dawn. There was so much jostling among the throng that the scaffold fell down killing twenty people. Lovat, nearly eighty years old by now, was amazed to see such a multitude.

'God save us, why should there be such a bustle about the taking off of an old grey head that cannot get up three steps without two men to support it?' he said. At the hastily resurrected scaffold, he accepted a drink of burnt brandy and bitters from the sheriff. He ascended the steps, supported by two warders, and presented Thrift with the customary purse. 'Here, sir, is ten guineas for you,' he said. 'Pray do your work well, for if you should cut and hack my shoulders, and I should be able to rise again, I shall be very angry with you.' He then ran his finger along the blade and muttered that he supposed it would have to do.

Before putting his head on the block, he quoted Horace, *'Dulce et decorum est pro patria mori'* (It is a sweet and proper thing to die for one's country) then Ovid in exculpation, *'Nam genus et proavos, et quae non fecimus ipsi, Vix ea nostra voco'* (For those things which were done either by our fathers or ancestors, and in which we ourselves had no share, I can scarcely call our own). He lay his head down on the block. This time, Thrift was on form and

Right: The Scottish Maiden, an early forerunner to the guillotine, preserved in the National Museum of Scotland

it is said that the head came off with a single blow. On the block inside the Tower of London, there are two deep grooves but it is thought the first was a practice stroke.

Thrift's axework made him no friends among the Jacobites living in London. They pelted him with stones and he was greeted with the derisive cry 'Jack Ketch' wherever he went. One evening in 1750, he was attacked by a gang of men near his home in Drury Lane. Running indoors, he grabbed a cutlass to defend himself. In the ensuing fray, one man fell dead: Thrift was arrested, tried, and sentenced to death. He was commuted to transportation to the American colonies but, before he went, the city of London realized they needed a competent hangman and Thrift was now a master of the rope if not of the axe. He was offered a free pardon if he resumed his profession but the man had already spent sixteen years on the scaffold and it all proved too much. He died on 5 May 1752.

Generally, the practice of beheading did not spread to Britain's colonies. Even in colonial North America, this was a rare form of execution. However the 1852 statute of the territory of Utah allowed a condemned man the right to choose between a firing squad, hanging, or beheading because the early Mormons, who arrived in 1847, believe in the doctrine of 'blood atonement,' citing Genesis, Chapter 9, Verse 6, which declares: 'Whoever sheds the blood of man, by man shall his blood be shed; for God made man in his own image'.

Abolition in Germany

On the Continent, decapitation was the most widespread form of capital punishment. In Germany, executioners used an axe with a broader blade (more like a meat cleaver) and a long handle which could be gripped with both hands. The last judicial beheading with an axe and a high block took place in 1935. The victims were Baroness Benita von Falkenhayn and Renate von Natzner who had been convicted of spying. The executioner, Carl Gröpler, wore a traditional tailcoat, top hat, and white gloves. The use of the axe was banned in 1938 by Adolf Hitler, who decreed that hanging or the guillotine should be used instead.

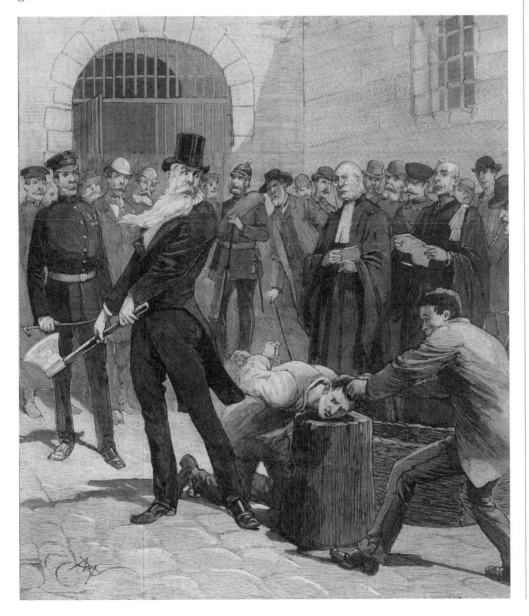

Left: Beheading in Berlin, with the executioner sporting the traditional German garb for the job

CHAPTER 3

Death By The Sword

Anne Boleyn famously did not face the axe. Henry VIII showed mercy and allowed her the privilege of being beheaded by sword. Unfortunately, none of his English executioners had any experience of using a sword, so a swordsman was brought over from Calais, then an English possession. For the occasion, the French executioner wore a special outfit – a tight black suit with a high, horn-shaped hat and a mask that covered part of his face – a costume paid for by the Constable of the Tower who was advanced one hundred French crowns (£23, nearly £7,500 in today's money) 'to give the executioner of Calays for his rewards and apparail'.

On 19 May 1536, the day of her execution, Anne rose at two in the morning, attended three masses, and had a little breakfast at seven. At eleven, the Constable of the Tower turned up at her apartments to escort her to Tower Green. While this was supposed to have been a private execution inside the precincts of the Tower, in attendance were the lords and ladies of the court, the officers of the Tower, the London Mayor, the city aldermen, and 200 Yeomen of the Guard. Henry VIII, for whom Anne had become an inconvenience, was nowhere to be seen.

The constable erected a scaffold on the green 'of such a height that all present shall see it'. It was five feet tall and strewn with straw under which the executioner stored his sword. Anne was wearing a black damask gown over a red underskirt with a white ermine collar and a small hat and she carried a golden prayer book and a white handkerchief. Her eyes were bright and it was plain to see she had been weeping. With the assistance of the constable, she mounted the scaffold. Eyewitnesses said Anne never looked more beautiful. Looking out across the crowd, she announced that she was innocent of any adulterous charges and that she had been a faithful wife and a loyal subject to the king.

She told the crowd:

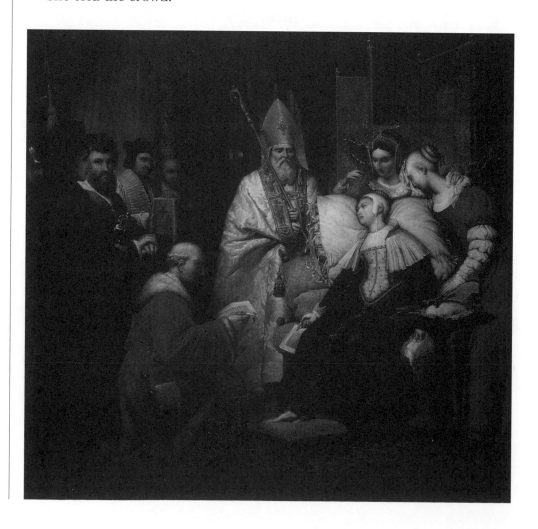

Right: Anne Boleyn hears the unwelcome news that Henry VIII has condemned her to death for treason

'Good Christian people, I have not come here to preach a sermon; I have come here to die, for according to the law and by the law I am judged to die, and therefore I will speak nothing against it. I am come hither to accuse no man, nor speak of that whereof I am accused and condemned to die, but I pray God save the king and send him long to reign over you, for a gentler nor a more merciful prince was there never, and to me he was ever a good, a gentle, and sovereign lord. And if any person will meddle of my cause, I require them to judge the best. And thus I take my leave of the world and of you all, and I heartily desire you all to pray for me.'

Her cape, hat, and jewellery were removed, her hair was tucked away under a white cap, and she handed her Bible to one of her ladies-in-waiting. Before kneeling down, she forgave her executioner and paid him to do his work well. There was no block: Continental executioners beheaded their victims with a horizontal stroke. Her lady-in-waiting blindfolded her with a linen handkerchief, by which time Anne was calm. An eyewitness said that 'she prepared to receive the stroke of death with resolution, so sedately as to cover her feet with her nether garments'. 'O Lord have mercy on me,' she said. 'To God I commend my soul. To Jesus Christ I commend my soul; Lord Jesus receive my soul.' The executioner pulled out his sword and signalled his assistant to walk towards Anne. Hearing this, she turned her head. The executioner swung, removing her head with a clean stroke and held it up, causing several ladies to faint.

Anxious that men would dishonour the body, the ladies of the court carried off the corpse and head wrapped in white cloth. It seems the executioner had neglected to order a coffin so the constable provided a wooden arrow chest from the nearby armoury and Anne was buried in a vault under the altar of the Chapel Royal.

German Swords

In most German provinces, the sword was favoured over the axe. The executioners used a two-handed sword with a blade that measured three to four feet long and two to two and a half inches wide, weighing around four pounds. An executioner's sword was decorated and needed no point so the end was rounded. A longitudinal groove or 'fuller' was cut into the sides near the handle so blood would flow towards the hilt rather than coagulate on the cutting edge. One example in the Royal Armouries had flowers etched on it. One side bore the slogan: '*Die Herren Strafen Unheil, Ich Exekutiere Ihr Urteil*' (The Lords punish evil, I execute their judgement'). The other side declared: '*Wan Ich das Schwert aufhebe, So Wünsche Ich dem Sunder das Ewige Leben*' (When I raise the sword, I wish the sinner everlasting life). The sword carried a picture of the wheel on which prisoners were broken for more serious offences. Others exemplars displayed the engraving of a gibbet.

Above: Execution of noble 'traitors' during the German *Bauernkrieg*, the Peasants' War, of 1525

The scabbards were made from wood and covered in leather with metal fittings and a smaller scabbard was attached to them. These contained small knives used to cut out the tongue or for disembowelling (depending on what sentence the courts had ordered). There would be no block, the reason being that even if the executioner made a downward stroke with his sword, its end would have become lodged in the wood before the neck had been severed. As in France, a horizontal stroke was used.

Despatching a prisoner using the sword required skill and, just as with the practitioners of the axe, inept executioners were often attacked by spectators: in 1509, an executioner was stoned to death in Prague Castle after a botched beheading.

Franz Schmidt, Specialist Executioner

The doyen of German executioners was a man called Franz Schmidt who ran the Nuremberg scaffold from 1573 to 1617 and was often 'on loan' to other jurisdictions that did not have their own executioner. His father had been an executioner in Bamburg. Unlike his English counterparts, Schmidt did not drink and lived modestly at the city's expense in a towerhouse on the stone bridge across the River Pegnitz.

Although Schmidt received an extra payment for each execution and torture in addition to his regular salary, he was also paid in the event of a last-minute reprieve. A common punishment in Germany was to allow a prisoner to believe that he had been condemned to death. Schmidt would knock on the prisoner's cell and make a formal apology while he tied the victim's hands and draped a white cloak around his shoulders. The prisoner would then be led to the courtroom to hear his sentence read aloud. Guarded by two mounted constables and accompanied by two chaplains, who administered the Sacraments, he would then be marched in procession to one of Nuremberg's two scaffolds: the *Hochgericht* (High Gallows) or the *Rabenstein* (Raven's Stone). If the prisoner was ill or old, he would be taken there in a cart; if the crime was particularly heinous, he would be bound and dragged to the scaffold on an ox hide or a wooden sled, risking injury if no one was on hand to raise his head clear of the cobbles. The assistant executioner followed with the coffin and some strong drink to fortify the victim during his coming ordeal.

Once the procession had made its way through the crowds gathered for the execution, the prisoner mounted the scaffold, built high up on a huge stone base so the crowd could get a good view. Many of the spectators were drunk and shouted abuse at the victim and the officials while cheering Schmidt on. He read out a proclamation promising retribution to anyone who tried to halt the event or avenge the death of the culprit. The condemned had one opportunity to address the crowd. Once the victim had prepared to meet his Maker, the executioner would twirl his sword in the air to build up speed for the final stroke. It was only then the prisoner discovered whether the blade simply flashed over the top of his head or sent him off with a *coup de grâce*. Even if he were reprieved, the scare would have created a lasting impression.

Schmidt did not bind his victims. They could flinch, sway, or pull away, making the first stroke ineffective, but he rarely had to take a second swing. In many cases, the prisoners begged to be beheaded rather than hanged. Decapitation was still considered a more honourable death than hanging, which was usually reserved for thieves and common criminals. In 1609, two daughters implored Schmidt to behead their father, as their fiancés would not marry them if he was hanged.

Anatomy was Schmidt's personal hobby. Like English hangmen, part of his job involved supplying corpses to medical schools, so he practised dissection on his victims and was also the municipal torturer. Though this may be seen as rather ghoulish, he seems to have been a humane man. Until 1513, women convicted of adultery in Nuremberg were buried alive. After that, they were drowned. Schmidt advocated that they should be beheaded for a quicker, more merciful death. He got his way even though critics maintained that weak women might faint and he might be obliged to finish them off on the ground. Consequently, Schmidt took the precaution of seating the condemned woman in a chair and beheading her with his sword from behind.

Unlike most English executioners, Schmidt could read and write and kept a diary. On 26 January 1580, he recorded beheading three women for infanticide. Twenty-two-year-old Agnes Lengin had strangled her baby and hid it in a garbage dump. Elizabeth Ernstin, also twenty-two, had staved in her child's skull and hidden the corpse in a trunk. Fifty-year-old (surely a mistake, according to Schmidt) Margaret Dorfflerin gave birth 'in the garden behind the fort' and left the baby to die in the snow. All three women were swiftly decapitated and had their heads nailed to the gallows 'no woman having been beheaded previously in Nuremberg'.

When Mistress von Ploben asked her maid, Margaret Bockin, to pick lice from her head, Bockin came at her from behind with an axe, killing her instantly. On 26 August 1580, she was brought to the scaffold by cart. Schmidt pulled at her flesh twice with red-hot pincers, before slicing her head off where she stood. Her body was buried under the scaffold and her head was fixed above it on a pole.

Anna Bischoffin had already been branded on both cheeks and whipped out of Würzburg. After pleading for her life on the grounds that she was pregnant, she was condemned to death for setting fire to a farm. Schmidt decapitated her, set her head up on the scaffold, and burned her body. Anna Peyelstainin 'had carnal intercourse with a father and son, both of whom were married, as was she, and similarly with twenty-one married men and youths, her husband colluding'. She was beheaded by the sword where she stood and her husband was whipped out of the town.

Barbara Wagnerin poisoned her husband's porridge with insect killer so she could marry Conrad Zwickel and took three spoonfuls herself to allay her spouse's suspicions. Nevertheless she was found out. The court discovered that Zwickel was not the only man in her life: she was having sexual relations with eighteen other men, some of whom were married. Schmidt beheaded rather than hanged her 'as a favour'. Agnes Rossnerin was also to be hanged but the 'poor creature... had a wry neck' so Schmidt beheaded her instead.

Mary Kursserin was not so lucky. On 10 January 1583, she and two other young prostitutes had suffered the pillory before being whipped out of the town. Mary was later caught stealing and had her ears excised before Schmidt could put a noose around her neck.

Left: An executioner displays the head of his latest victim to the crowd, c.16th century

During his forty-four years in office, Schmidt executed 360 felons, forty-two of whom were women. His busiest year was 1580 when he executed twenty people. These included two murderers broken on the wheel plus two more murderers and nine thieves who were hanged.

There were many other memorable entries in his diary. In 1576, he recorded executing one Hans Payhel 'who committed three murders; two years ago, I cut off his ears and flogged him; today I beheaded him at Forchheim', a town eighteen miles north of Nuremberg. On 6 August 1579, he beheaded three thieves. Frau Dieterich turned up to the event only to discover that one of them was her husband whom she 'embraced and kissed, for she had not known her husband had been arrested, nor that he was that sort of fellow'. On 10 August 1581, Schmidt despatched 'George Schörpff, a lecher, guilty of sodomy with four cows, two calves, and a sheep. I beheaded him for unnatural vice at Velln; his body was burnt afterwards, together with a cow'. It is not clear why only one cow was burned.

Schmidt also recorded the extraordinary case of George Praun who had robbed a fellow traveller. In Vienna, he had stolen a suitcase full of clothes and a pair of white stockings. Schmidt decapitated him on 14 September 1602 but, when his head was placed on a stone, 'it turned several times as if it wanted to look around, moved its tongue and opened its mouth as if it wanted to speak, for a good half-quarter hour – I have never seen the like of this'.

Promiscuity was condemned in men as well as women. On 23 June 1612, Schmidt executed Andrew Feverstein who ran a school with his father. Feverstein junior had preyed on sixteen schoolgirls in his care. Schmidt once again beheaded him as 'a favour'.

Andrew Brunner was convicted of blasphemy for blaming a thunderstorm on the Almighty. Schmidt tore his tongue out and fixed him to the scaffold so the crowd could abuse him but it was not all doom and gloom. The pickpocket and murderer Hans Ditz sang all the way to his beheading while the ever-optimistic horse thief Hans Porstner offered five florins and a pair of shoes to the assistant executioner if he would trade places with him.

Below: German execution sword, of the type used by Franz Schmidt. Note the rounded end: this was a cutting rather than a stabbing weapon

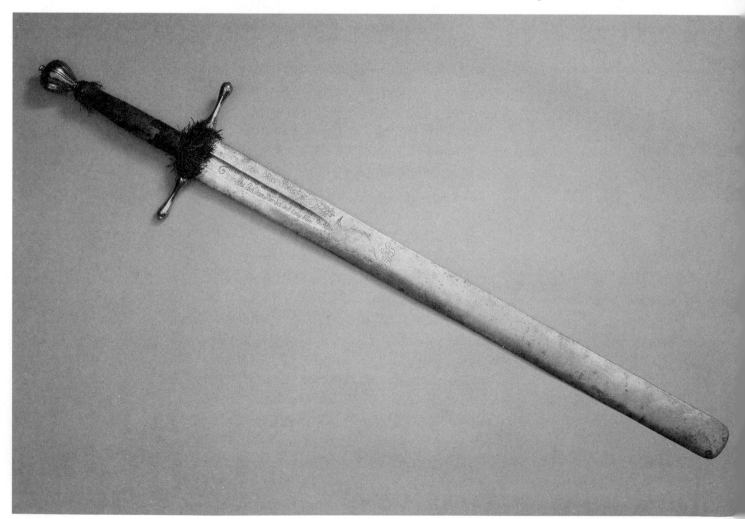

Incompetents on the Scaffold

In 1617, Schmidt retired from his profession, returned to Bamberg where he died in 1634. He was given a dignified funeral attended by a number of city dignitaries. Some executioners after Schmidt were also competent. On 20 October 1645, Matthias Perger managed to take off not just a felon's head but his two hands as well when the fellow raised his arms at the last moment. Another succeeded in taking off two heads with a single blow. Later at Leipzig, the executioner organized a choir to accompany the spectacle. The choirmaster was none other than Johann Sebastian Bach.

Some, though, were dazzlingly poor at their job. One such was Valtin Deusser, an executioner at Bamberg in 1641, where he was due to despatch an unfortunate woman. The city records report that:

'the poor sinner was weak and ill, so she had to be led to the scaffold. When she sat down on the chair, Master Valtin the executioner walked around her like a cat walks around hot broth. He held the sword a span from her neck, took aim, and struck the blow, but missed her neck and struck off a slice of her head as big as a coin, knocking her from the chair. Then the poor soul got up quicker than she had sat down, this blow having done no harm to her. Then she started to beg to be let go, as she had been so brave. But to no avail. She had to sit down again. The assistant then wanted to take the sword from Master Valtin and strike her himself, but the master would not permit this and struck her again himself. The second blow was a little stronger and she fell from the chair. Then he cut off her head as she lay on the scaffold. The executioner received his reward as he went. He would have been stoned to death if the town guard and their arms had not rescued him. As it was, much blood was already streaming from his head.'

On 27 June 1665, another executioner was sacked after a woman was clumsily executed : 'after five strokes she still cried out, and finally her head was cut off as she lay on the ground'. In 1717, Johann Widman nearly took off his assistant's hands when the man who was condemned struggled at the last moment.

Although public execution was banned in Germany in 1851, the death of one Bertha Zillman in 1893 was witnessed by a number of journalists. She was sentenced for poisoning her husband, although the court heard evidence that he beat both her and their children. The execution was scheduled to take place on 31 October at Plötzensee Prison in Berlin at eight o'clock in the morning. Her hair was put up in a bun and her dress cut down to her shoulders, though she was given a shawl to cover herself. When the warden went to fetch her, she was prostrate with fear and had to be helped to the block by two male warders. She silently dropped the shawl and, with one swing, was beheaded by her executioner. Three minutes later, it was all over.

A Deadly Family

The Sanson family provided seven generations of Parisian executioners spanning the years from the era of the sword as the preferred method of execution through to the French Revolution's introduction of the guillotine. Some family members, however, were not as competent as others.

On 3 June 1699, Angeline-Nicole Tiquet arrived at the scaffold of Charles Sanson de Longval in the Place de Grève. She had been found guilty of conspiring to murder her husband after five shots had been fired at him outside the house of a female acquaintance believed to be his lover. It was also known, however, that Madame Tiquet had numerous gentleman friends and rumours circulated that she was behind the assassination attempt.

Lieutenant Defitta, the prosecutor assigned to investigate the case, was himself a former beau of Madam Tiquet. Nevertheless he had her tied to a bench on her back and a cow's horn was inserted in her mouth. Eight pots of water were assembled, which she would be forced to drink unless she confessed. One pot was enough: she confessed and named Jacques Moura the porter as her co-conspirator. He was to be hanged while Madame Tiquet was to be beheaded due to her higher social status.

A reprieve was expected but none came. It was said that Monsieur Tiquet went to Versailles with their two children and threw himself at the feet of Louis XIV. The king refused clemency but allowed Monsieur Tiquet to keep his wife's property rather than have it forfeited to the Crown. On the appointed day, Madame Tiquet, in a white dress, and her confessor were loaded onto a tumbril. A thunderstorm delayed the proceedings but they arrived at the Place de Grève in time to see Moura hang.

Sanson assisted Madame Tiquet up onto the scaffold. After a short prayer, she asked calmly: 'Sir, will you be good enough to show me the position I am to take?' 'Kneel down with your head up and your hair lifted from your neck,' said Sanson. 'Take care not to disfigure me,' said the beautiful Angelique. Sanson swung the sword but the first stroke sliced off her ear and cheek. The force of the blow threw her forward and his two assistants had to pick her up and hold her in place. He struck again but still her head did not come off. By this time, the crowd was becoming agitated and violent. Henri-Clement Sanson, Sanson de Longval's descendant, wrote in 1862: 'The blood spurted out but the head did not fall. A cry of horror rose from the crowd. Sanson de Longval struck again; again, the hissing of the sword was heard but the head was not separated from the body. The cries of the crowd were becoming threatening. Blinded by the blood that spurted with every stroke, Sanson brandished his weapon a third time with a kind of frenzy. At last the head rolled at his feet. His assistant picked it up and placed it on the block, where it remained for some time; and several witnesses asserted that even in death it retained its former calmness and beauty.' However, this case is not as bad as that of the amateur headsman who took twenty strokes of the sword to put the Comte de Calais to death in 1626.

The great Charles-Henri Sanson was also known to miss his aim from time to time. In 1766, he was entrusted with the execution of the Comte Thomas Arthur de Lally-Tollendal, who himself had had Hindus, suspected of being spies, blown from the barrel of a gun when he was commander of the French forces in India, thereby rallying the Indians to the British. Thirty-five years earlier, Lally-Tollendal and some fellow officers were lost in the suburbs of Paris one night when they came upon a house where there was a ball. They knocked on the door and were invited in. It was being held to celebrate a wedding and they danced until dawn. As they were leaving, they asked the bridegroom his name and he replied: 'Jean-Baptiste Sanson'.

Some of the officers were disturbed that they had spent the night in the company of a family of executioners but Lally-Tollendal was fascinated and asked if he could see the tools of the trade. Jean-Baptiste complied and found him particularly interested in his 'Sword of Justice' (the execution sword). It was some thirty-three inches long and about two and a half inches wide, with a blunt tip. A simple guard protected its double-handed grip and a heavy pommel gave it the necessary balance. Like its German equivalent, it had a wheel engraved on one side and the word *Justica* on the other. Lally-Tollendal held up the sword and took several practice swings with it. Could it remove a man's head with a single blow? he asked. Jean-Baptiste said that it could and promised that if Lally-Tollendal was ever on the scaffold, he would not suffer.

By the time Lally-Tollendal came to the Place de Grève, Jean-Baptiste Sanson had already suffered a stroke and was partially paralyzed down one side. The execution was going to be performed by his son, Charles-Henri. The old man accompanied his son to the scaffold, where he loosened the prisoner's bonds and removed the iron gag that had been put on him by the jailers at the Bastille. The condemned man protested his innocence and prayed. Once his hands were untied, he handed his handsome gold jacket, made for him in India, to Jean-Baptiste. 'Now you can strike,' he said to Charles-Henri.

Lally-Tollendal's hair had not been cut so it obstructed the blade and the sword cut into the comte's cheek and jaw instead, breaking his teeth. Lally-Tollendal fell to the ground. He sprung back to his feet and glared at Jean-Baptiste. A quick-witted assistant grabbed the comte by the ears as Jean-Baptiste Sanson suddenly recovered his strength. He grabbed the blooded sword from his son and, before the cry of horror that had risen from the crowd had subsided, removed Lally-Tollendal's head.

Charles-Henri made amends when executing the Chevalier de la Barre later that year. The handsome, nineteen-year-old chevalier had set his heart on marrying a particular girl. However, her guardian, the Lieutenant Criminel of Abbeville, had arranged a more favourable match. To get the unwanted chevalier out of the way, he accused him of failing to salute passing monks, a blasphemous act which in itself warranted a sentence of death.

On the scaffold, Sanson asked the chevalier to kneel. He refused. 'But it is the custom for criminals to kneel,' insisted Sanson. 'I cannot; I am no criminal,' said the chevalier. 'Strike me as I am…Now be quick.' Sanson swung his sword, this time with astonishing accuracy. It passed through the neck cleanly without dislodging the head and the body remained standing for a few moments. An eyewitness reported that Sanson had said 'shake yourself – the job is done' to the upright corpse. To the amazement of all that witnessed the feat, it was only when the body had crumpled at last that the head rolled across the scaffold. Charles-Henri Sanson went on to oversee the introduction of the guillotine.

Beheading in the Far East

In most European countries, the sword was the preferred method of execution but it was also popular in the Far East. However, there was one marked difference: beheading was regarded as a dishonourable end in that part of the world. In death, it was considered important for the body to remain intact, so dividing the head from the body and disposing of the parts separately was looked upon as shameful.

In 1691, the Dutch traveller Engelbert Kaempfer witnessed the public execution of two criminals in Japan:

'Early in the morning of the execution, the governor of Nagasaki sent notice to our director to keep himself with the rest of the Dutchmen in readiness to see the criminals executed. About an hour later, numerous flocks of people arrived, our interpreters, landlords, cooks, with the sheriffs and other officers of justice, in all to the number of at least 200 people. Before the company was carried a pike with a tablet, whereon the crime for which the criminals were to suffer was specified in large characters. Then followed the two criminals surrounded by bailiffs. The first was the buyer of the stolen goods, a young man of twenty-three years of age, very meanly clad, upon whom the stolen property, camphor, was found. The second was a well-looking man, about forty years of age, who suffered only for having lent the other, formerly a servant of his, the money to buy it with. One of the bailiffs carried an instrument upright, formed like a rake, but with iron hooks instead of teeth, to be made use of if any of the malefactors should attempt to make his escape as it easily catches hold of one's clothes. Another carried another instrument, proper to cut, to stab, and to pin one fast to the wall. Then followed the two officers of the governor's court with their retinues, to preside at this act, and at some distance came two clerks. At the scene I saw the two criminals in the middle of the place, one behind the other, kneeling, their shoulders uncovered and their hands tied behind their backs. Each had his executioner standing by him, the one a tanner, for tanners in this country do the office of executioners, the other his best friend and comrade, who he earnestly

desired as is the custom in this country, by doing him this piece of service, to confirm the friendship he had always had for him. The spectators stood around as promiscuously as they pleased, but I, with my Japanese servant, crowded as near one of the malefactors as we could. The minute the Dutch were all assembled at the place of execution, a signal was given and, in that instant, both executioners cut off the criminal's head with a short scymitar, in such a manner that their bodies fell forward to the ground. The bodies were wrapped up, each in a coarse rush mat, and both their heads put together in a third, and so carried away to a field not far from Nagasaki where, it was said, young people tried their strength and the sharpness of their scymitars upon the dead bodies by hacking them into small pieces. Both heads were fixed on a pole, according to custom, and exposed for view for seven days.'

Above: Execution by beheading of pirates, French Indochina c.19th century. The board in front of the condemned lists his crimes, and his sentence

Thomas Taylor Meadows, the interpreter to the British Consulate in China, witnessed a mass beheading during the Taiping Rebellion of 1851. Back in London, he told the Royal Asiatic Society that some 400 people had been put to death in the same place over the last eight months and that a fire of fragrant

Right: Chinese peasants, converts to Catholicism, are executed during China's nineteenth-century Boxer Rebellion

sandalwood was burning near where the mandarins who were superintending the executions sat to conceal the stench of the decomposing heads.

'The criminals were brought in, the greater number walking, but many carried in large baskets of bamboo, each of which was attached to a pole and borne by two men. We observed that the strength of the men so carried was altogether gone, either from excess of fear or from the treatment they had met with during their imprisonment and trial. They fell powerless together as they were tumbled out on the spots where they were to die, and were immediately raised up to a kneeling position and supported thus by the man who stands behind them. The following is the manner of decapitation. There is no block, the criminal simply kneels with his face parallel to the earth, thus leaving his neck exposed in a horizontal position. His hands, crossed and tied behind his back, are grasped by the man behind who, by tilting them up, is enabled in some degree to keep the neck at the proper level. Sometimes, though very rarely, the criminal resists to the last by throwing back his head. In such cases, a second assistant goes in front and, taking the long Chinese tail or queue, normally kept rolled in a knot on top of the head, by dragging it, pulls the head out horizontally.

'The sword usually employed is only about three feet long, inclusive of a six-inch handle, and the blade is not broader than an inch and a half at the hilt, narrowing

and slightly curving towards the point. It is not thick and is in fact the short and by no means heavy sabre worn by the Chinese military officers when on duty.

'The executioners, who are taken from the ranks of the army, are indeed very frequently asked by the officers to "flesh their maiden swords" for them. This is called "kae kow", opening the edge, and is supposed to endow the weapon with a certain power of killing.

'The sabre is firmly held with both hands, the right hand in front, with the thumbs projecting over and grasping the hilt. The executioner, with his feet planted some distance apart to brace himself, holds the sabre for an instant at the right angle to the neck, about a foot above it, in order to take aim at a joint in the vertebrae; then, with a sharp order to the criminal of "Don't Move!" he raises it straight before him, as high as his head, and brings it down rapidly with the full force of both arms, giving additional force to the cut by dropping his body perpendicular to a sitting position at the moment the sword touches the neck. He never makes a second cut, and the head is seldom left attached even by a portion of skin, but is completely severed.

'On the present occasion, thirty-three of the criminals were arranged in rows with their heads towards the south, where we were standing. In the extreme front, the narrowness of the ground only left space for one man at about five yards from us; then came two in a row, then four, five, etc. At the back of all, about twenty-five yards from us, the chief criminal, a leader of a band, was bound up to the cross. The executioner, with the sleeves of his jacket rolled up, stood at the side of the foremost criminal. He was a well-built, vigorous-looking man of middle size: he had nothing of the brutal or ferocious look in his appearance, as one is led to expect, but on the contrary had good features and an intelligent expression.

'When all was ready, the man stood firm, with his legs somewhat apart and his eyes on the military officer superintending. On hearing the word "Pan!" [Punish!], he threw himself into the position described above and commenced his work. Either from nervousness or some other cause, he did not succeed in severing the first head completely, so that after it fell forward with the body, the features kept moving for a while in ghastly contortions. In the meantime, the executioner was going rapidly on with his terrible task. He appeared to get somewhat excited, flinging aside a sword after it had been twice or thrice used, seizing a fresh one held ready by an assistant, and then throwing himself by a single bound into position by the side of the next victim. I think he cut off thirty-three heads in somewhat less than three minutes, all but the first being completely severed.

'Most of the trunks fell forward the instant the head was off; but I observed that in some three or four cases, where the criminals were men apparently possessing their mental and physical capacities at full strength, the headless body stood quite upright, and would I am certain have sprung in the air had they not been retained by the man behind; till, the impulse given in the last instant of existence being expended, a push threw them forwards to their heads...I may add that of the thirty-three men decapitated, no one struggled or uttered any exclamation as the executioner approached him.

'Immediately after the first body fell, I observed a man put himself in a sitting posture by the neck, and, with a business-like air, commence dipping in the blood a bush of rush pith. When it was well saturated, he put it carefully by on a pile of the adjacent pottery, and then proceeded to saturate another bunch. This so-saturated rush pith is used by the Chinese as medicine. When all the executions were over, a lad of about fifteen or sixteen, an assistant or servant I presume of the executioner, took a sabre and, placing one foot on the back of the first body, with the left hand seized hold of the head (which I have already said was not completely cut off) and then sawed away at the severed portion of the neck till he cut through it. The other bodies were in the meantime being deposited in coffins of unplaned deal boards. When that was nearly finished, the southern door being opened, we hastened to escape from a sight which few will choose to witness a second time without a weighty special cause.'

The Chinese now use a single bullet in the back of the head at mass executions.

Around the World

British diplomats were not always mere witnesses to public beheadings. In January 1824, the British governor of Sierra Leone, Sir Charles M'Carthy, set out with a small, advanced unit to quell an uprising of the Ashante tribe. His advance was slowed down by heavy rains and he soon found himself surrounded by a superior force. It was then he discovered that the ammunition boxes they were carrying contained, not the ball cartridges they needed – but biscuits! The band gallantly continued to play the national

Right: Modern-day execution by the sword, in the Yemen. A number of Arabic countries, including Saudi Arabia, still practise executions by this method

anthem as they were overrun by the enemy. The survivors were marched into an Ashante village and ceremonially decapitated. The heads of Sir Charles M'Carthy and his staff were taken to Kumasi, the Ashante capital, where they were bedecked with gold and jewels and displayed at the Royal Treasury. The top of M'Carthy's skull was cut off and used by the Ashante kings as a drinking cup – a great honour apparently.

The Saudis continue their tradition of beheading. In the early 1990s, Saed Al Sayaf, the Saudi chief executioner, said: 'To chop off the heads of men I use a special sword, following the writings of the prophet Mohammed, while I use a gun to execute women. When the job is done, I get a sense of delight and thank God for giving me this power'. Since then, the Saudis have made a move towards equal rights and both men and women are now decapitated. By the end of 2004, some thirty-four women were publicly beheaded.

In Saudi Arabia, public beheading is the punishment for rape, murder, sodomy, drug trafficking, armed robbery, apostasy, and other offences. These public spectacles continue into the twenty-first century: in 2002, forty-five men and two women were beheaded; in 2002, fifty-two men and one woman; in 2004, thirty-five men and one woman.

The condemned are fed tranquillizers before being taken by police van to a public square or an open car park after the midday prayers. The police clear traffic from the square and a sheet of blue plastic some sixteen feet square is laid out on the ground. The condemned man or woman is led to the centre of it by a police officer and made to kneel facing the direction of Mecca. The victims are dressed in their own clothes but are blindfolded and barefoot with their hands cuffed behind their back and their feet shackled.

The prisoner's name and crime are announced to the crowd by an Interior Ministry official. A policeman then hands a traditional scimitar to the executioner who raises it and takes two or three practice swings before approaching the victim from behind. A jab in the back with the tip of the sword makes the prisoner raise their head. Then comes the deadly blow.

It usually takes one swing to remove the head. A good swordsman can send it flying as far as two or three feet. A doctor is on hand to staunch the blood pouring from the neck and it is he who sews the head back on after the paramedic has collected it and handed it to him. Finally, the corpse is wrapped in the blue plastic sheet and taken away to be buried at the prison cemetery in an unmarked grave.

Jihadists in Iraq, Afghanistan, and elsewhere use beheading to dispose of their victims. This is now done as publicly as possible by posting digital footage of the gruesome events on the Internet. The British engineer Ken Bigley and the American contractor Nick Berg were victims in Iraq in 2004. Both deaths were very public and their perpetrators no doubt considered them executions, but as no form of judicial procedure ever took place, their deaths can be categorized as cold-blooded murders.

CHAPTER 4

The Road to Tyburn

The Origins of Hanging

Hanging originated as a method of execution about 2,500 years ago in ancient Persia. It was used for male criminals as women were strangled at the stake for the sake of decency. Hanging became widespread because it was easy to perform: all you needed was a tree and a long piece of rope. It was also an effective deterrent because it could be performed publicly without the bloody horror of more gruesome methods which might put people off watching. Hanging was also recommended in the Old Testament in Deuteronomy Chapter 21, Verse 22–23: 'And if a man has committed a crime punishable by death, and he is put to death, and you hang him on the tree, but you shall bury him the same day, for a hanged man is accused by God; you shall not defile your land which the Lord your God gives you for an inheritance'.

British Hanging

In antiquity, hanging was considered a form of death befitting cowards. Consequently, it was seen as a dishonourable way to die. In England, from Anglo-Saxon times it was the traditional method of execution, until beheading was introduced in the eleventh century by William the Conqueror (*see* Chapter Two). Although executions were carried out throughout the country, the most usual place for the public execution of common criminals became Jack Ketch's Tree at Tyburn in London (where Marble Arch now stands) though there were also gallows elsewhere in London: in Soho Square, Bloomsbury Square, Smithfield, St Giles in Holborn and Blackheath, and on Kennington Common and City Road in Islington. Occasionally people were publicly hanged outside the place where they had committed a particularly heinous crime.

The first person to be executed at Tyburn was William 'Longbeard' Fitzrobert in 1196, who had led a rebellion against the tax being levied to ransom Richard the Lionheart from Henry VI of Austria. When the rebellion failed, William sought sanctuary in St Mary-le-Bow in the city of London but Hubert de Burgh, the Archbishop of Canterbury, who was also Justiciary of the Kingdom (prime minister and chief justice rolled into one) ordered his men to set fire to the church and force Longbeard out. Ironically, de Burgh later sought sanctuary there himself, but when this proved controversial, he fled to Wales.

The place of execution was known as Tyburn Fields, a large area of rough ground through which the River Ty flowed ('burn' means 'river' or 'stream' in Old English). A stand of elm trees grew on the banks of the Ty and the Normans considered the elm to be the 'tree of justice'. At least 50,000 people met a violent death on this 'tree of justice' at Tyburn between 1196 and 1783, the year of the last execution.

The Short Drop

Tyburn was well situated on the main roads into London from the north and the west. The open ground meant that huge crowds could congregate to watch the spectacle, and the hangings also acted as a deterrent for those heading into the city.

The elm trunks were later used to carry fresh water from the Ty into the city. The Middlesex Gallows, built on the stream's western shore, featured a single beam where ten prisoners could be hanged at a time. The condemned criminal would be made to climb a ladder. The hangman would attach the noose to the beam, then 'turn off' the felon so he swung free. Once the horse and cart was introduced to transport prisoners from Newgate Prison, it, too, was used in the executions. Felons would stand on the cart with their hands tied behind their backs. Once their necks had been secured to the beam, the

hangman would pull a cap down over each prisoner's face and whack the horse on the flanks. The animal would take off, taking the cart with it, leaving the condemned criminals swinging. After half an hour, the bodies would be cut down and disposed of.

The 'long-drop' method of execution, which snapped the felon's neck and killed him instantly, was not used until the late nineteenth century, when hangings were confined to behind prison walls. Throughout the history of public hangings in Britain, the 'short-drop' method was used. Sometimes the rope was as short as three feet. In order to snap the neck of a man weighing fourteen stone, an eight-foot drop was needed; for an individual weighing eight stone, the drop was ten feet. The hangmen of Tyburn used a noose with a running knot which would be tightened around the felon's neck, effectively strangling them. This process could take up to twenty minutes. As an act of kindness, friends, servants, and sometimes even the hangman himself pulled on the victim's legs to hasten their demise, but this did not always work.

When 22-year-old Anne Green was hanged in the Cattle Yard at Oxford on 14 December 1650 for murdering her own child, people came forward to pinch her breasts and 'amuse themselves' by hanging from her legs. After lifting her up, they pushed all their weight down on her and she fell with a

Above: Plaque on London's Oxford Street, showing the location of the old Tyburn gallows

forceful jerk. The court usher attending the execution feared the rope might break and asked the crowd to leave her alone. After about half an hour, they cut her down and she was taken to Dr William Petty who would later use her body in his anatomy lectures at the local university. When a group of medical students assembled for the dissection and opened up the coffin, they noticed that the young woman was still breathing. They poured her a hot drink and warmed her up by putting her to bed. After an hour, she could talk; a week later, she was as good as new. The court reprieved her and she moved out to the country taking her coffin with her. She later married, had three children, and lived for another fifteen years.

Once the felon had been hanged, women would sometimes rush forward to press their faces or breasts against the still-twitching hands. This bizarre practice was thought to cure blemishes. The sweat of a dead criminal was also thought to be beneficial and mothers would hold up sickly infants at public executions. Lengths of hangman's rope and shavings from the gallows were also thought to have a curative effect.

Below: Execution procession: convict is taken to the gallows at Tyburn, England, eighteenth century

The Tyburn Procession

In 1571, the single beam at Tyburn was replaced by the famous 'triple tree' which had three beams that could each accommodate eight people, so a total of twenty-four people could be hanged at a time. During the reign of James I, around 150 people were hanged in a year. By the 1700s, up to forty victims a day were being despatched and Tyburn fairs were held every six weeks.

If the condemned criminals were of high rank they were held in the Tower of London. Otherwise they languished in the filthy dungeons of Newgate Prison which stood on the current site of the Old Bailey. London merchant Robert Dow left an annuity to pay for a man to ring a hand bell outside Newgate the night before an execution, reminding the condemned of their imminent death and urging them to repent. He believed this would help the condemned prepare themselves for their journey into the afterlife. Victims were also subjected to a hellfire-and-damnation sermon in a chapel draped in black with their coffins on a table in front of them while the rest of the congregation ogled them.

Originally, criminals were dragged from Newgate to Tyburn behind a horse but this often resulted in premature death and deprived the crowds of the spectacle they had come to see. Later victims were therefore dragged on an ox skin or a sled but it seemed more sensible to bring them from Newgate by cart along with their coffin and a pastor to comfort them on the way to their execution.

Notorious criminals often played to the cheering crowds by dressing up for the occasion as if they were going to a wedding or some other important event. Their first stop was the Church of St Sepulchre, where the bell was tolled twelve times and offenders were handed a bunch of posies. The bell would then be rung once more at the end of the execution. A pigeon released at Tyburn would carry news of the event. The tolling of the bell was also paid for by Robert Dow's annuity of a modest one pound, six shillings, and eight pence (£1.33 or £185 in today's money). The practice was brought to an end with the hanging of Mary Pearcy on 23 December 1890. A guest at the Viaduct Hotel near St Sepulchre fell ill and the vicar was asked to suspend the ringing of the bell. As the procession to Tyburn had ended more than a hundred years earlier, the tradition was never renewed.

The condemned were given a jug of ale at the hospital of the Church of St Giles-in-the-Field and stopped at every pub on the way to their execution, most famously at the White Hart in Drury Lane. This is the origin of the expression 'one for the road'. Each publican would give the condemned free ale as they attracted crowds and were good for business. One Captain Stafford asked for a bottle of wine on his way to the gallows. He had an urgent appointment to keep, he said, but would pay for it on the way back. It is said that one teetotaller refused refreshment and was hanged moments before a messenger arrived on horseback with a reprieve. Had he stopped for a drink, his life would have been spared. Although this tradition was ended in 1750, a pub named The Bowl was built on the site of the hospital.

Hampered by huge crowds, the procession along Oxford Road (now Oxford Street) could take hours to reach its destination. Popular prisoners were showered with flowers while unpopular ones were pelted with rotten vegetables and stones. The whole affair had a carnival atmosphere about it with crowds singing and chanting, and street vendors selling gingerbread, gin, and oranges.

Jack Sheppard taken from Newgate.

Blueskin attempting to Rescue Jack Sheppard on Holborn Hill.

Right: Engraving by George Cruickshank of highwayman Jack Sheppard's procession to the Tyburn gallows

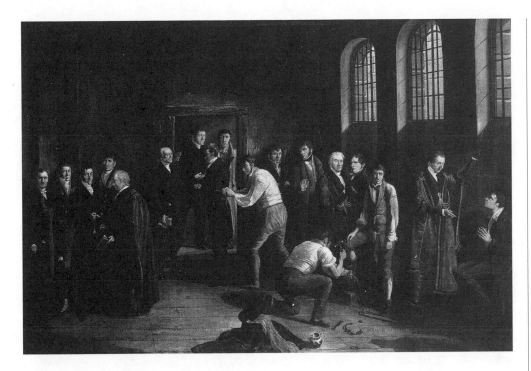

Left: Chained: a convict has fetters put on his legs in Newgate Prison, the oldest prison in London

The Spectacle of the Gallows

Around the gallows were wooden stands where spectators paid two shillings (10p) for a good view. The largest stand with the best view was Old Mother Proctor's Pews, named after its owner. On one occasion – the execution of an earl – she made £500 but things could go awry. In 1798, pew owner Mammy Douglas hiked up her prices for the hanging of the traitor Dr Henesey and the public duly paid up but a riot broke out when the criminal was given a last-minute reprieve. The stands were demolished and Mammy Douglas narrowly escaped with her life.

When the cart carrying the condemned arrived, cries of 'hats off' and 'down in front' would be heard so everyone got a good view. Bawdy songs were sung along with a revivalist hymn which carried the line 'Oh my, I think I've got to die'.

A priest would recite a prayer and the condemned were invited to publicly confess their crimes. Some gave long self-justification speeches; others seized the moment to abuse the authorities, the hangman, the priest, or the crowd. The smuggler John Biggs informed the crowd: 'I never was a murderer, unless killing fleas and such-like harmless little cruelties fall under the statute. Neither am I guilty of being a whoremaster, since females have always had the ascendancy over me, not I over them. No, I am come here to swing like a pendulum for endeavouring to be too rich, too soon.'

Proceedings were rarely as dignified at Tyburn as they were at the Tower of London. The hangman 'Jolly Jack' Hooper, who officiated from 1728 to 1735, was renowned for his clown-like antics on the scaffold. Jack Ketch, who was as poor a hangman as he was an axeman, was told by James Turner: 'What, dost thou intend to choke me? Pray, fellow, give me more rope! What a simple fellow is this. How long have you been executioner, that you know not where to put the knot?' As the cap was being pulled down over his face, Turner spotted a pretty girl in the crowd, blew her a kiss and, as the rope tightened, said: 'Your servant, mistress'.

Another felon with an eye for the ladies was Tom Austin. When the chaplain asked him whether he had anything to say before he was hanged, he replied: 'Nothing, only there's a woman yonder with some curds and whey. I wish I could have a pennyworth of them before I'm hanged 'cos I don't know when I'll see any again'.

The hangman was entitled to keep the clothes of the dead. These were normally stripped from the body once it was cut down and before it was sent to the anatomist, but in 1447 five men were stripped – ready for hanging – when their pardons came through. The hangman refused to return their clothes and they were forced to walk home naked.

Hannah Dagoe, an Irish girl who robbed a friend in Covent Garden in 1763, put on quite a show. She terrorized her fellow inmates at Newgate and stabbed a man who had given evidence against her. In the cart on the way to Tyburn, she paid no attention to the Catholic priest who was with her. Under the gallows, she wriggled her hands free and punched the hangman so violently that she knocked him down. She then dared him to hang her and took her revenge on him by giving away her clothes. Stripping off her hat, cloak, and dress, Hannah threw them into the crowd. The hangman even struggled to get the noose around her neck, but as soon as he had done so she threw herself off the cart with such violence that she broke her neck and died instantly.

The bodies of victims were also the hangman's property. Although obliged to sell the corpses of murderers to surgeons for dissection purposes, the executioner sometimes sold them back to the families if they offered a better price. It was often difficult to keep the body intact as the crowd would grab pieces as macabre souvenirs. On 18 December 1758, a riot broke out when the medics fought the family for possession of the victim's body – however, the mob won and carried the corpse away in triumph. The hangman would also be allowed to cut up the rope that was used in the execution and sell bits off in the pubs on Fleet Street.

At the Scene of the Crime

Felons were sometimes hanged near the location of their crime. On 21 January 1664, Samuel Pepys recorded in his *Diary:*

'Up, and after sending my wife to my aunt Wight's, to get a place to see Turner hanged, I to the 'Change'; and seeing people flock to the City, I enquired, and found that Turner was not yet hanged. So I went among them to Leadenhall Street, at the

end of Lyme Street, near where the robbery was done; and to St Mary Axe, where he lived. And there I got for a shilling to stand upon the wheel of a cart, in great pain, above an hour before the execution was done; he delaying the time by long discourses and prayers, one after another in hopes of a reprieve; but none came, and at last he was flung off the ladder in his cloak. A comely-looking man he was, and kept his countenance to the end; I was sorry to see him. It was believed there were at least 12,000 to 14,000 in the street.'

Above: Eighteenth-century anatomy lesson. The bodies of those hanged at Tyburn frequently ended up as surgical demonstrations

Triple murderer Sarah Malcolm was hanged in Fleet Street between Fetter Lane and Mitre Court, near where she had murdered her mistress and two fellow servants. The 22-year-old showed no contrition and, when the bellman came to Newgate, threw him a shilling to buy wine. At her execution though she acted with dignity and resignation. She fainted and was revived with difficulty. 'Oh, my mistress, my mistress,' she said. 'I wish I could see her.' As the cart pulled away, Sarah commended her soul to Christ. Laughing Jack Hooper was affected by this. Either he believed she was innocent or had been touched by the newspaper stories about her fall from grace. Soon after, John Thrift took over as hangman, despatching thirteen people on his first day as executioner.

By 1759, the Tyburn gallows was beginning to impede traffic on its way in and out of London so the triple tree was demolished and a 'moving gallows' used instead. Timbers from the old gallows were sold to local pubs as barrel stands though some were retained by the Tyburn Convent as local relics of martyred Catholics. A toll gate was later installed at the site which proved more unpopular than the gallows.

Below: Earl Ferrers hanged for the murder of his land agent, 5 May 1760. A very unusual execution: condemned aristocrats were usually beheaded on Tower Hill

A Nobleman on the Gallows

A new method of hanging was introduced the following year. On 5 May 1760, Laurence Shirley, the fourth Earl Ferrers, was executed at Tyburn. A drunken, violent man, he had quarrelled with the agent who ran his estates and shot him dead. Imprisoned in the Tower, he was tried by the House of Lords at Westminster Hall and found guilty. He asked to be beheaded on Tower Hill, but their lordships decided that he should hang like a common criminal at Tyburn, after which his body would be given over to the anatomists for dissection. He asked to be hanged with a silken cord, instead of a hemp rope, as befitted his rank. This request, too, was denied. The only novel introduction at his hanging would be the use of a trapdoor. A platform had been raised about eighteen inches above the scaffold with a hatch that measured about three feet square. The earl was meant to stand on it as the noose was put around his neck. The hatch would then open, killing him. That was the theory of it at least.

For his execution, Ferrers wore the same white suit with silver trimmings that he had worn at his wedding. He travelled from the Tower to Tyburn in his own carriage but the crowds were so thick that the journey took nearly three hours. 'They have never seen a lord hanged before,' he remarked to the sheriff.

The procession comprised a detachment of grenadier guards, a company of life guards, lines of constables, numerous city officials, coaches full of friends and well-wishers, and a hearse. No one wanted to miss the spectacle. The earl, nonchalantly chewing on tobacco, waved to the crowds. When the horse of the cavalryman that was escorting him got its leg caught in the wheel of the coach and threw off its rider, Ferrers remarked, 'I hope there will be no death today but mine'.

According to Horace Walpole, the funeral procession 'was stopped at the gallows by a vast crowd, but [he] got out of his coach as soon as he could, and was but seven minutes on the scaffold, which was hung with black…The mob was decent, admired him, and almost pitied him'. Whatever unpleasantness there was took place on the scaffold itself. After handing over his watch to the sheriff, along with five guineas to the chaplain, Ferrers mistakenly gave another five to the assistant hangman rather than to the headman, Thomas Turlis. The two men came to blows until the sheriff finally stepped in and gave Turlis his money.

The earl did receive some privileges as befitted his social status. His hands were tied in front with a piece of black sash instead of behind him with ordinary cord. Turlis guided him onto the raised part of the scaffold which was covered with black baize. 'Am I right?' asked the earl. Turlis nodded and pulled down the white cap over his face. He operated the mechanism and Ferrers dropped down but there had been a grave miscalculation. 'As the machine was new, they were not ready at it,' commented Horace Walpole.

'His toes still touched the stage and he suffered a little, having had time by their bungling to raise his cap; but the executioner pulled it down again, and they pulled his legs so that he was soon out of pain, and quite dead in four minutes.'

After an hour, the body was taken down. This resulted in another brawl between the hangmen. 'The executioners fought for the rope,' said Walpole, 'and the one who lost it, cried'. The rope was, of course, valuable booty. The body was laid out in a coffin lined with white satin and taken to the Surgeon's Hall, where it was cut open and put on display for the next three days before being handed back to the family for burial.

Hangmen

Turlis was also known to have squabbled with the condemned. On 27 March 1771, he was suddenly struck in the face and injured during an altercation as he was hanging five men at Tyburn. Five days later, he collapsed in the cart on his way back from a hanging at Kingston, Surrey, and died.

Edward Dennis took over the job of hangman. However, when the anti-Catholic Gordon Riots – instigated by the fanatical Protestant Lord George Gordon – broke out, Dennis was seen smashing up a chandler's shop. He was arrested in the Blue Posts pub at the Southampton Buildings, Holborn, and charged with being one of the ringleaders. Dennis was sentenced to death even though he broke down at his trial and begged for mercy. As his death would have plunged his family into penury, he asked that his son be allowed to succeed him as executioner. The newspapers made much of the story of a son hanging his own father. In the event, the authorities had a problem of their own: fifty-nine rioters had been condemned but there was nowhere to hold them prisoner because Newgate Prison had burned down. Ned Dennis's talents were much needed at this moment and he was reprieved so that he could help hang his fellow rioters!

Now that the gallows were mobile, Dennis could carry out his work in the city: at Bishopsgate in Bow Street and in Bloomsbury Square, as well as at Whitechapel, Oxford Road, and Old Street. It is thought he officiated at the hanging of three rioters (William M'Donald, Mary Roberts, and Charlotte Gardiner) on Tower Hill, making them the last people to be executed there.

The Decline of Tyburn

By the end of the eighteenth century, the area around Tyburn was beginning to flourish. In 1771, the Dowager Lady Waldegrave began building a grand house nearby and the newspapers reported that 'through the particular interest of her ladyship, the place of execution will be moved to another spot'. There were moral objections to public executions as they attracted too

many spectators. 'Sir, executions are intended to draw spectators,' said Dr Johnson. 'If they do not draw spectators, they don't answer their purpose.'

On 7 November 1783, John Austin became the last man to be hanged at Tyburn. Convicted of robbing and injuring a man, he was despatched by the old horse-and-cart method. Again, the execution was bungled. The knot slipped around the back of Austin's neck, prolonging his death.

Tyburn Lane became Park Lane, Tyburn Road became part of Oxford Street, and Tyburn Gate became Cumberland Gate. Meanwhile the home of public hanging in London became the street outside the newly rebuilt Newgate Prison at the Old Bailey. Edward Dennis and William Brunskill, his assistant, performed their first executions on 9 December 1783. They kept a new mobile gallows in a shed at Newgate and hauled it out whenever it was needed.

Above: The Marble Arch end of Oxford Street, early nineteenth century, formerly known as the Tyburn Turnpike. Although executions ceased in the area in 1783, it retained a poor reputation for a long time afterwards

Above: Debtor's Door at Newgate Prison. Executions were carried out here after Tyburn was abandoned

Hanging at Newgate

Eight feet wide and ten feet long, with two parallel crossbeams that could carry ten criminals, there was even room on the moveable gallows for city officials to sit down. It featured a trap system which had not developed much further from the one that had been used unsuccessfully on earl Ferrers. The ten individuals despatched that day had to be strangled slowly because the ropes were much too short – a technical problem that was not rectified for another ninety years! The bodyweight-to-rope length ratio that was required to snap the neck cleanly was finally worked out behind closed doors. Until then, it was considered better for a felon to strangle slowly at the end of a short rope rather than have his head torn off by a longer one.

The local residents were not pleased with the new venue. A newspaper reported that 'the inhabitants of the neighbourhood, having petitioned the sheriffs to remove the scene of the execution to the old place, were told that the plan had been well considered, and would be persevered in'. The truth was that the residents of the well-to-do houses being erected around Hyde Park simply held more sway. The regular processions from Newgate to Tyburn disrupted trade in the newly built-up shopping area and the wild

'Tyburn fairs' that were held along one of the main thoroughfares into the city gave visitors a bad impression. Far fewer spectators could fit into the area around the Old Bailey so the crowds were easier to control and the residents soon got used to the idea when they began renting out rooms with windows overlooking the scaffold whenever there was a hanging. By 1840, it cost £25 (over £15,000 in today's money) to rent a window with a good view and the keeper of Newgate Gaol would entertain distinguished guests with a lavish breakfast of devilled kidneys and brandy on the day of the executions.

Bungled Executions

Three years after the gallows had been moved to Newgate, Dennis died in his apartment at the Old Bailey and William Brunskill took over. At his first solo performance – hanging seven offenders before a large crowd – he took a bow but became a little accident prone. On 5 June 1797, he was executing Martin

Below: Legendary eighteenth-century highwayman Jack Sheppard, who escaped twice from Newgate Prison, turns his hand to a spot of house-breaking

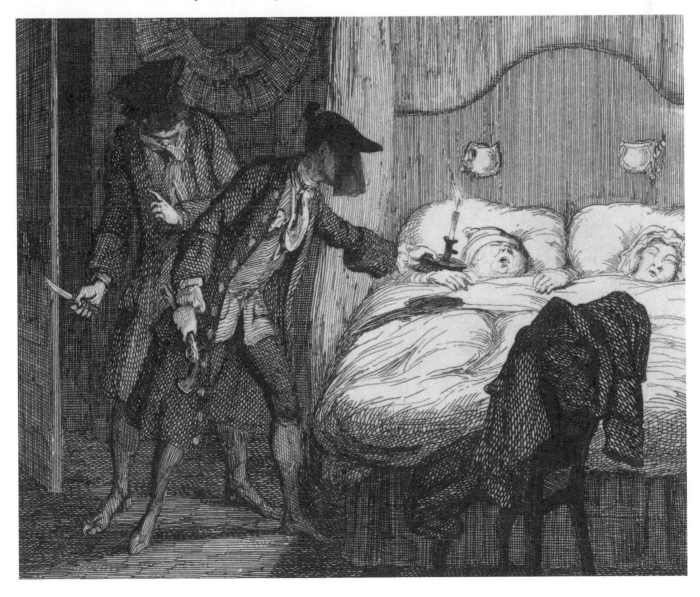

Clench and James Mackley who claimed to be innocent of murdering Sydney Fryer. As Brunskill and his assistant John Langley were about to pull down their caps, the trapdoor gave way and the two condemned men tumbled down the hatch along with their executioners and priests. The felons were stopped by the ropes while the others landed in a heap at the bottom of the hatch.

A Newgate hanging went even more disastrously wrong when John Holloway and Benjamin Haggerty went to the scaffold on 22 February 1807 still protesting their innocence over the murder of John Cole Steele on Hounslow Heath five years earlier. They were joined by Elizabeth Godfrey who had been convicted of the wilful murder of Richard Prince the previous Christmas, by stabbing him in the eye with a pocketknife. They were hanged together. According to the *Newgate Calendar*:

> 'the crowd which assembled to witness this execution was unparalleled, being, according to the best calculation, nearly forty thousand; and the fatal catastrophe which happened in consequence will for long cause the day to be remembered. By eight o'clock not an inch of ground was unoccupied in view of the platform. The pressure of the crowd was such that, before the malefactors appeared, numbers of persons were crying out in vain to escape from it; the attempt only tended to increase the confusion. Several females of low stature who had been so imprudent as to venture among the mob were in a dismal situation; their cries were dreadful. Some who could be no longer supported by the men were suffered to fall and were trampled to death. This also was the case with several men and boys. In all parts there were continued cries of "Murder! Murder!" particularly from the females and children among the spectators, some of whom were seen expiring without the possibility of obtaining the least assistance, everyone being employed in endeavours to preserve his own life.
>
> 'The most affecting scene of distress was seen at Green Arbour Lane, nearly opposite the debtors' door. The terrible occurrence which took place near this spot was attributed to the circumstance of two piemen attending there to dispose of their pies. One of them having had his basket overthrown, which stood upon a sort of stool with four legs, some of the mob, not being aware of what had happened, and at the same time being severely pressed, fell over the basket, and the man at the moment he was picking it up, together with its contents. Those who once fell were never more suffered to rise, such was the violence of the mob.
>
> 'At this fatal place, a man of the name of Herrington was thrown down, who had by the hand his youngest son, a fine boy about twelve years of age. The youth was soon trampled to death; the father recovered, though much bruised, and was amongst the wounded in St Bartholomew's Hospital. A woman who was so imprudent as to bring with her a child at the breast was one of the number killed. Whilst in the act of falling, she forced the child into the arms of the man nearest to her, requesting him, for God's sake, to save its life. The man, finding it required all

his exertion to preserve himself, threw the infant from him, but it was fortunately caught at a distance by another man who, finding it difficult to ensure its safety or his own, got rid of it in a similar way. The child was again caught by a man, who contrived to struggle with it to a cart, under which he deposited it until the danger was over, and the mob had dispersed. In other parts, the pressure was so great that a horrible scene of confusion ensued, and seven persons lost their lives by suffocation alone. It was shocking to behold a large body of the crowd, as one convulsive struggle for life, fight with the most savage fury with each other; the consequence was that the weakest, particularly the women, fell a sacrifice. A cart which was overloaded with spectators broke down, and some of the persons who fell from the vehicle were trampled underfoot, and never recovered. During the hour that the malefactors hung, little assistance could be afforded to the unhappy sufferers; but after the bodies were cut down, and the gallows removed to the Old Bailey Yard, the marshals and constables cleared the street where the catastrophe occurred and, shocking to relate, there lay nearly one hundred persons dead, or in a state of insensibility, strewed

Above: 'Under the Scaffold, or The Hangman's Pupils' a satirical look at the popular fascination with public executions, c.18th century

round the street! Twenty-seven dead bodies were taken to St Bartholomew's Hospital, four to St Sepulchre's Church, one to the Swan, on Snow Hill, one to a public house opposite St Andrew's Church, Holborn; one, an apprentice, to his master's; Mr Broadwood, pianoforte maker, to Golden Square. A mother was seen carrying away the body of her dead boy; Mr Harrison, a respectable gentleman, was taken to his house at Holloway. There was a sailor-boy killed opposite Newgate by suffocation; he carried a small bag, in which he had some bread and cheese, and was supposed to have come some distance to behold the execution. After the dead, dying, and wounded were carried away, there was a cartload of shoes, hats, petticoats, and other articles of wearing apparel picked up. Until four o'clock in the afternoon, most of the surrounding houses had some person in a wounded state; they were afterwards taken away by their friends on shutters or in hackney coaches. The doors of St Bartholomew's Hospital were closed against the populace. After the bodies of the dead were stripped and washed, they were ranged round a ward on the first floor on the women's side; they were placed on the floor with sheets over them, and their clothes put as pillows under their heads; their faces were uncovered. There was a rail along the centre of the room: the persons admitted to see the shocking spectacle went up on one side of the rail and returned on the other. Until two o'clock, the entrances to the hospital were beset with mothers weeping for sons, wives for their husbands, and sisters for their brothers, and various individuals for their relatives and friends.

'The next day (Tuesday), a coroner's inquest sat in St Bartholomew's Hospital, and other places where the bodies were, on the remains of the sufferers. Several witnesses were examined with respect to the circumstances of the accident, which examination continued till Friday, when the verdict was, "That the several persons came by their death from compression and suffocation."'

Other things could go wrong. On 2 January 1827, a bookseller in Holborn named Charles Thomas White was found guilty of attempting to burn down his own house for the insurance and was sentenced to death. On the scaffold, he struggled violently with the hangman James Foxen and his assistant Thomas Cheshire. When Foxen moved to operate the drop, White freed his hands and wrenched off his cap. As the drop fell, he jumped up and grabbed the rope. An eyewitness reported that

'during his exertions, his tongue had been forced from his mouth, and the convulsions of his body and the contortions of his face were truly appalling. The cries from the crowd were of a frightful description and they continued until the executioner had forced the wretched man's hand from the rope and, having removed his feet from the platform, had suffered his whole weight to be sustained by the rope. The distortions of his countenance could even now be seen by the crowd, and as he remained suspended with his face uncovered, the spectacle was terrific. The hangman at length terminated his sufferings by hanging onto his legs, and the unhappy wretch was seen to struggle no more.'

Facing page: Another satirical look at public executions, this time by George Cruikshank, a vociferous opponent of the practice

The Movement for Abolition

The movement to end public hanging in England lasted fifty years, with an increasing number of people rallying to its banner, until it finally achieved its aim in 1868. It was started one morning in the spring of 1818 when the artist George Cruikshank, illustrator of many books by Charles Dickens, was strolling in the city and came across the gallows still hanging with corpses. Two of the bodies were female and looked barely older than sixteen. When he asked a bystander what the girls had done, he was informed that they had been hanged for trying to forge a £1 note.

Shocked, Cruikshank drew his own version of a £1 note and replaced the head of Queen Victoria with a row of corpses hanging from the gallows. When his drawing was published, it caused great outrage. The Bank of England ceased to issue £1 notes for a time. Under public pressure, Sir Robert Peel, the Home Secretary, was finally forced to abolish the death penalty for minor crimes in 1832.

Charles Dickens himself, a true nineteenth-century liberal, lent his weight to the campaign. After seeing the execution of Maria and Frederick Mannings for murdering Maria's lover, Patrick O'Connor, in Horsemonger Lane, outside the Surrey County Gaol on 13 November 1849, he wrote to *The Times* saying:

'I believe that a sight so inconceivably awful as the wickedness and levity of the immense crowd collected at that execution this morning could be imagined by no man, and could be presented in no heathen land under the sun. The horrors of the gibbet and of the crime which brought these wretched murderers to it faded in my mind before the atrocious bearing, looks, and language of the assembled spectators. I came upon the scene at midnight…As the night went on, screeching and laughing, and yelling in strong chorus of parodies on Negro melodies, with substitutions of "Mrs Manning" for "Susannah" and the like were added to these. When the day dawned, thieves, low prostitutes, ruffians, and vagabonds of every kind, flocked on the ground, with every variety of offensive and foul behaviour…When the sun rose brightly, it gilded thousands upon thousands of upturned faces, so inexpressibly odious in their brutal mirth or callousness that a man had cause to feel ashamed of the shape he wore. When these two miserable creatures, who attracted all this ghastly sight about them, were turned quivering into the air there was no more emotion, no more pity, no more thought that two immortal souls had gone to judgement, than if the name of Christ had never been heard in this world.'

Although it was a degrading spectacle – Mrs Manning fainted while being pinioned and had to be revived with brandy – according to *The Times* the two 'died almost without a struggle'. The crowd, who had been so raucous the night before, were well behaved, too: 'scarcely a hat or a cap was raised while the drop fell; and the bodies of the murderers had hardly ceased to oscillate with the momentum of their fall before the spectators were hurrying from the scene.'

Public hangings were abolished in 1868. The last one took place outside Newgate Prison on 26 May of that same year. The man hanged was an Irish terrorist called Michael Barratt who had blown up the Clerkenwell House of Detention killing six people. A drunken crowd stayed up all night to witness the execution. They cheered wildly when the scaffold was brought out at dawn. More people – mainly young women and children – began to arrive. By the time a bell was sounded at eight o'clock in the morning to announce the arrival of the condemned man, the crowd stretched back as far as Smithfield.

According to *The Times,*

'with the first sound of the bells came a great hungry roar from the crowd outside, and a loud, contained shout of "Hats off", till the whole dense, bareheaded mass stood white and ghastly-looking in the morning sun, and the pressure on the barriers increased so that the girls and women in the front rank began to scream and struggle to get free. Amid such a scene as this and before such a dense crowd of white faces, Barrett mounted the steps with the most perfect firmness. This may seem a stereotyped phrase, but it really means more than is generally imagined. To ascend the ladder with one's arms and hands closely pinioned would be at all times difficult, but to climb a ladder to go to a certain death might try the nerves of the boldest.

'Barrett walked up coolly and boldly. His face was as white as marble, but still he bore himself with firmness, and his demeanour was as far removed from bravado as from fear. We would not dwell on these details but from the singular reception he met as he came upon the scaffold. There was a partial burst of cheers, which was instantly accompanied by loud hisses, and so it remained for some seconds, till as the last moment approached, the roars dwindled down to a dead silence. To neither cheers nor hisses did the culprit make the slightest recognition. He seemed only attentive to what the priest was saying to him and to be engaged in fervent prayer.

'The hangman instantly put the cap over his face and the rope round his neck. Then Barrett turning spoke though his cap and asked for the rope to be altered, which the hangman did. In another moment, Barrett was a dead man. After the bolt was drawn and the drop fell with a loud boom which always echoes from it, Barrett never moved. He died without a struggle. It is worthy of remark that a great cry rose from the crowd as the culprit fell – a cry which was neither an exclamation or a scream, but it partook of the sound of both. With the fall of the drop, the crowd began to disperse but an immense mass waited till the time for cutting down came, and when nine o'clock struck, there were loud calls of "Come on, body snatcher!" and "Take away the man you've killed!" The hangman appeared and cut down the body amid a storm of yells and execrations as has seldom been heard even from such a crowd. There was nothing more to be seen, so the concourse broke up with its usual concomitants of assault and robbery.'

The Noose in France

As well as in England, hanging was the most common method of execution in France until the guillotine was introduced in 1792. Almost every town and village in the country had a permanent gibbet with rotting corpses or skeletons hanging from it. Not surprisingly, the most famous was in Paris and stood on a hill called Montfaucon to the north of the city, near the main road that led to Germany. The name of the hill became the name of the gallows.

According to the writer Paul Lacroix,

'this celebrated place of execution consisted of a heavy mass of masonry, composed of ten or twelve layers of rough stones, and formed an enclosure of forty feet by twenty-five or thirty. On the upper part there was a platform reached by a stone stairway, the entrance to which was closed off by a massive door. On three sides of this platform rested ten square pillars about thirty feet high, made of stone blocks one foot thick. These pillars were joined to one another by the double bars of wood fastened to them and bore iron chains three and a half feet long, from which criminals were suspended. Underneath, halfway between them and the platform, other bars were placed for the same purpose. Long and solid ladders riveted to the pillars enabled the executioner and his assistants to lead up criminals or to carry up corpses destined to be hung there. Lastly, the centre of the structure was occupied by a deep pit, the hideous receptacle of the decaying remains of the criminals.

'One can easily imagine the strange and melancholy aspect of this monumental gibbet if one thinks of the number of corpses continually attached to it which were feasted upon by thousands of crows. On a single occasion, it was necessary to replace fifty-two chains which were useless, and the accounts of the city of Paris proved that the expenses of executions were more heavy than that of the maintenance of the gibbet.'

Condemned criminals were taken there in a cart – sitting or standing – with their backs to the horse, the confessor by their side, and the executioner at the back. Felons had three ropes around their neck: two '*tortouses*' with slipknots and the third '*jet*' which was used to pull them off the ladder. At the gallows, the executioner would climb the ladder backwards, pulling the felon up behind him by means of the ropes. The *tortouses* would be tied to the gibbet before the felon was pulled off the ladder with the *jet*. Finally, the executioner would speed up the strangulation by placing his feet on the victim's tied hands and jerking the rope.

Montfaucon was used not only for executions but also for exposing corpses brought from other parts of the country. The place was guarded by archers to keep away witches who supposedly used the brains of criminals to make potions. The mutilated remains of felons who had been beheaded, quartered, or boiled dangled from wicker baskets or leather sacks and would often hang for a considerable length of time. The body of Pierre des Essarts, who was beheaded in 1413, hung from the gallows for three years before

finally being returned to his family for a proper burial. Montfaucon fell into disuse in the early seventeenth century and was replaced by a smaller gallows further out of town.

As at Tyburn and Montfaucon, huge crowds gathered to participate in the lively atmosphere at executions in other places. Sometime the multitudes were so great that the authorities closed the gates to stop more people from coming in. Contemporary reports showed that spectators got through wagonloads of food and drink at these events.

Above: The gibbet at Montfaucon, Paris's principal place of execution before the introduction of the guillotine

Hanging in the USA

Colonial America also adopted the gallows for executing common criminal,s and public hangings continued well into the twentieth century. There were, of course, many semi-public lynchings by the Ku Klux Klan in the deep South but these were extra-judicial killings and qualified as murders rather than executions. When the train robber 'Black Jack' Ketchum was hanged in front of a crowd of cowboys and townsfolk in Clayton, New Mexico, in 1901, he bounded up the thirteen steps to the gallows, two at a time. The hanging was to be by the merciful 'long-drop' method but, unfortunately, the hangman got his calculations wrong. With the noose around his neck, the moustachioed bandit shouted to the crowd: 'I'll be in hell before you start breakfast, boys'. He turned to the sheriff: 'Let her rip'. How right he was – as he plunged through the trapdoor, the noose tore his head from his body.

A similar thing happened in Washington DC in 1880, at the execution of James Stone who, ironically, was condemned to death for attacking his wife and sister-in-law with a razor, practically decapitating them both. When the hangman opened the trap, his head was plucked from his body. After the cap was removed, Stone's features seemed to be composed, his lips were still moving, and his heart continued beating for another two minutes.

Such accidents turned the American population against the use of hanging. Since the re-introduction of the death penalty in 1976, this form of capital punishment is now an option in only two states – Washington and Delaware – along with lethal injection.

The last official public hanging in the United States took place in Galena, Stone County, Missouri, in 1937. In August 1934, travelling salesman Pearl Bozarth had stopped to give hitchhiker Roscoe 'Red' Jackson a lift, and even bought him a meal in Branson, Missouri, before Jackson killed him. At six in the morning on 21 May 1937, Jackson was brought out onto a scaffold in a stockade in Galena's main square. Some 400 invitations had been originally sent out to witness the spectacle but the crowds that now sat in trees and other vantage points had reached 2,000 or more, including a great many women and children.

Invited to make a farewell speech, the condemned man said, 'This is the end of me. I'm the cause of all this public confusion. I guess it's asking too much for everyone concerned to forgive me, but I want all of you to know that I meet death with a heart free of all hatred. I blame no one for this but myself, and the law is merely doing its duty.' He then prayed with a Catholic priest and was heard asking Jesus for mercy. The noose was put around his neck and tightened. 'Be good, folks,' he cried out.

The trap was sprung and he dropped to his death. After that incident, Missouri began using the gas chamber instead due to the behaviour of onlookers at public executions. A week after the hanging of Roscoe Jackson, *The New York Times* reported that 'within the past year there have been several

public hangings by county officers which have shocked and embarrassed Missourians who believe that an execution is no occasion for a Roman holiday. In at least three instances, small communities have become carnival spots for the day as hundreds of persons for miles around came to town to see the spectacle.'

Neighbouring Kentucky maintained public hanging on its statute books until 1938, and the last public execution in the United States was that of Rainey Bethea, a 22-year-old black man, in Owensboro, Daviess County, Kentucky. Bethea was hanged in front of a white mob numbering over 1,00 people. A habitual drunk and petty criminal, he had been found guilty of the rape and murder of Lischa Edwards, a seventy-year-old white woman. Although Bethea had murdered Edwards, he was charged only with her rape, as this was a crime punishable by hanging, rather than the electric chair. The execution sprang to national prominence when it was discovered that the new sheriff of Daviess County was a woman, Florence Thompson: it would be her job to hang Bethea. In the event, a more experienced hangman named Hash deputized for Thompson. When the trap was sprung, Bethea dropped eight feet and died instantly. Reports of the crowd surging forward to grab 'souvenirs' from the dead man appear to be exaggerated, although they were instrumental in the abolition of public execution in the United States.

Above: The hanging of Rainey Bethea, the last public execution in the United States, 14 August 1936

A Traytors head

C H A P T E R   5

Hanging, Drawing, and Quartering

'That you be led to the place from whence you came, and

from thence be drawn upon a hurdle to the place of

execution, and then you shall be hanged by the neck and,

being alive, shall be cut down, your privy members shall be

cut off, and your entrails taken out of your body and, you

living, the same to be burnt before your eyes, and your head

to be cut off, your body divided into four quarters, and the

head and four quarters to be disposed of at the pleasure of

the king's majesty. And the Lord have mercy on your soul.'

Death sentence for hanging, drawing and quartering, England

In England, the ultimate execution method for men who committed high treason was hanging, drawing, and quartering. (It was considered indecent at the time to mutilate a woman's body in this way, so female traitors were burnt at the stake.)

The hurdle mentioned above in the death sentence was a piece of fencing made from interwoven branches which was dragged by a horse with the condemned man tied to it. The prisoner would be hanged by the 'short-drop' method to ensure his neck was not broken and, left dangling in this manner, he was already half-dead from strangulation. He would then be cut down and laid out on a wooden bench, at which point the executioner would remove the genitals and toss them into a brazier. The stomach would be opened up, and the entrails extracted and burned. Finally, the heart was removed, the head severed, and the body quartered. At some point during this grisly ordeal, the victim would die of asphyxiation, shock, or damage to his vital organs. If the condemned man had fomented a rebellion, the four pieces of his body were taken to different corners of the kingdom to ensure that everyone was well aware of what lay in store for traitors. The head would be displayed at the end of a spike either on a castle's battlements or on London Bridge, as a grim warning to all.

This form of public execution was thought to have been devised in 1241 specifically to punish William Maurice, the son of a nobleman who had turned to piracy. It was certainly used in 1283 on David Ap Gruffydd, the last native Welsh prince to claim the title of Prince of Wales. After an attack on the English garrison at Hawarden, Clwyd, he was tried for treason in Shrewsbury and sentenced 'to be drawn to the gallows as a traitor to the king who made him a knight, to be hanged as the murderer of the gentleman taken in the Castle of Hawarden, to have his limbs burnt because he had profaned by assassination the solemnity of Christ's passion, and to have his quarters dispersed through the country because he had in different places compassed the death of his lord the king'.

The Scottish patriot Sir William Wallace famously suffered the same fate in 1305. Convicted of treason – although he pointed out that he had never sworn allegiance to the English king – he was dragged through the streets of London tied to the tails of several horses. The following day, he was conducted to a scaffold in Smithfield where the grisly sentence was carried out. His quartered remains were sent to Perth, Stirling, Berwick-upon-Tweed, and Newcastle-upon-Tyne, where his severed sword-hand was already on display. Wallace's head was stuck on a spike and displayed on London Bridge 'in sight of both land and water travellers'. As this was the first recorded instance, Londoners flocked to see the head in their hundreds. Before going on display, heads were parboiled in a big cauldron filled with spices in a room called Jack Ketch's kitchen at Newgate Prison. This practice discouraged seagulls from pecking away at the flesh.

Martyrs to their Faith

Between 1535 and 1681, some 105 Catholic martyrs were publicly hanged, drawn, and quartered at Tyburn for failing to convert to Protestantism. Guy Fawkes and his Gunpowder Plot co-conspirators had planned to blow up King James I of England (VI of Scotland) inside the Houses of Parliament in 1605 and were sentenced to this death. Robert Winter, Thomas Bates, John Grant, and Sir Everard Digby were despatched near St Paul's Churchyard on 30 January 1606. According to one eyewitness, the executioner said 'here is the heart of a traitor' as he held up Digby's heart whereupon Everard, who, though heartless, was apparently not dead, replied, 'thou liest'.

The following day, Thomas Winter, Ambrose Rookwood, Robert Keyes, and Guy Fawkes were dragged to the Old Place Yard in front of the Houses of Parliament. Mounting the scaffold, Winter begged forgiveness for his crime and declared that he died a true Catholic. It was said that he was as pale as death as he mounted the ladder and was cut down after a swing or two, hauled to the quartering table, and despatched mercifully.

Rookwood made a long speech admitting his guilt and asking for God's mercy. He bequeathed his family to the king for whom he wished a long and

Above: William Wallace, leader of the thirteenth-century Scottish rebellion, on trial for his life before Edward I of England

Iustitia

SUPPLICIUM
De octo coniuratis sumtum in Britann
diebus 30. et 31. Jan. Styl. vet. Anno
sumtum quidem separatim de quate
Sed tamen propter eandem omnino Supp
rationem, hac tabella coniunctim expressu

Left: The execution of Guy Fawkes and the 'Gunpowder Plotters' of 1605, after their failed attempt to assassinate King James I and restore Catholicism to England

Right: King James I of England (James VI of Scotland) in full regal attire. In many ways a moderate and successful king, James nevertheless made enemies in Parliament and amongst his Catholic subjects

happy life. He also asked God to make the king a Catholic. When he was cut down, he was dead.

Keyes made no speech. He simply climbed straight up the ladder and jumped off it in a desperate attempt to break his neck and get his execution over and done with relatively painlessly. It failed as the rope broke and he was dragged alive and conscious to the quartering table for the most horrendous mutilation.

Lastly, there was Fawkes, who was contrite. He beseeched 'all Catholics never to attempt such a bloody act, being a course which God did never favour or prosper'. He had been terribly tortured and could hardly scale up the ladder but, with the help of the executioner, he managed to climb up high enough to break his neck with the fall. Mercifully, he was dead when he was finally dismembered.

The quartered bodies of these conspirators were displayed over the city gates while their heads appeared on London Bridge. The cost of setting them up on spikes was twenty-three shillings and nine pence (£1.19 or £150 in today's money). The bill is kept in the Tower of London to this day.

Quartering the Regicides

In August 1660, after being restored to the throne, Charles II passed the Act of Free and General Pardon, Indemnity, and Oblivion which forgave anyone who had supported Oliver Cromwell and his Republican government. The only exception were those individuals who had signed his father's death warrant. A special court was appointed and, in October 1660, the regicides were brought to trial, summarily found guilty, and sentenced to be hanged, drawn, and quartered.

The first to die was Major-General Thomas Harrison who, though he had fought for Parliament during the Civil War and signed Charles I's death warrant, later fell out with Cromwell and was duly imprisoned. A contemporary publication called *An Exact and Impartial Account of the Indictment, Arraignment, Tryal, and Judgment (according to Law) of Twenty-Nine Regicides, The Murderers of His Late Majesty Of Most Glorious Memory...* carried this description of his death:

'On Saturday, 13 October 1660, betwixt nine and ten of the clock in the morning, Mr Tho. Harrison or Major General Harrison, according to sentence, was upon a hurdle drawn from Newgate to the place called Charing Cross; where within certain rails lately there made, a gibbet was erected, and he hanged with his face looking towards the Banqueting-House at Whitehall, (the place where our late Sovereign of Eternal Memory was sacrificed) being half-dead, he was cut down by the common executioner, his privy members cut off before his eyes, his bowels burned, his head severed from his body, and his body divided into quarters, which were returned back

to Newgate upon the same hurdle that carried it. His head is set on a pole on the top of the south-east end of Westminster-Hall, looking towards London. The quarters of his body are in the like manner exposed upon some of the city gates.'

One of those who saw Harrison being executed was Samuel Pepys who wrote in his *Diary*:

'I went out to Charing Cross to see Major-General Harrison hanged, drawn, and quartered, which was done there, he was looking as cheerful as any man could do in that condition. He was presently cut down, and his head and heart shown to the people, at which there was great shouts of joy.'

The great surprise was how long Harrison survived the ordeal. After he 'was cut down alive, and his entrails were taken out of his body, he rose up and had strength enough left to strike the executioner'. This was probably the

self-styled 'Squire' Edward Dun who brutally taunted his victims.

Over the following week, nine more regicides – John Carew, John Cook, Hugh Peters, Thomas Scot, Gregory Clemen, Adrian Scroop, John Jones, Francis Hacker, and Daniel Axel – were despatched publicly in a similarly hideous fashion.

On 20 October, Samuel Pepys wrote:

'This afternoon going through London and calling at Crowe's, the upholster's in St Bartholomew's, I saw the limbs of some of our new traitors set upon Aldersgate, which was a sad sight to see; and a bloody week this and the last have been, there being ten hanged, drawn, and quartered.'

By then, others who had signed the death warrant were themselves dead, but that did not mean they would escape retribution. John Bradshaw, Thomas Pride, Henry Ireton, and Oliver Cromwell were posthumously subjected to a farcical trial for high treason. Found guilty, their bodies were dug up in January 1661 and hanged in chains at Tyburn.

Right: Oliver Cromwell, Lord Protector of England and prime mover in the sending to trial of Charles I

Jacobite Rebels

Three more men were hanged, drawn, and quartered after the Jacobite Rebellion of 1715. They were Captain William Kerr, Captain John Gordon, and John Dorrell, all of whom were executed at Tyburn on 7 December of that year. The 1745 Jacobite Rebellion yielded another ninety-one sentences of hanging, drawing, and quartering. Twenty were carried out at Carlisle; six at Brampton; and seven at Penrith. Another twenty-two took place at York the following year, along with seventeen at Kennington Common, the place of execution for the County of Surrey, now known as Kennington Park, near Camberwell. One of them was 37-year-old Francis Townley, a colonel in the Manchester Regiment of the Jacobite army which surrendered to the Duke of Cumberland after briefly holding Carlisle in late 1745. He was executed in

July of the following year. A contemporary account reported this: 'After he had hung for six minutes, he was cut down, and, having life in him, as he lay on the block to be quartered, the executioner gave him several blows on the breast, which not having the effect designed, he immediately cut his throat; after which he took his head off; then he ripped him open, took out his bowels, and threw them into the fire, which consumed them, then he slashed his four quarters, put them with the head into a coffin, and they were deposited till Saturday, 2 August, when his head was put on Temple Bar and his body and limbs suffered to be buried.' The head was stolen from there and secretly held by the Townley family until 1945 when it was buried in their vault in Burnley.

The executioner made sure Townley was already dead by the time the disembowelling began and gradually the more revolting parts of the sentence were mitigated. When Dr Archibald Cameron was executed at Tyburn on 7 June 1753 for his part in the 1745 rebellion, he was left hanging for twenty minutes before being cut down, by which time he was almost certainly dead. He was then beheaded but it is unclear whether the rest of the mutilation went ahead. His remains were buried in the Savoy Chapel.

When the spy François Henri De La Motte was executed at Tyburn on 27 July 1781 for conspiring to murder George III, he was hanged for nearly half an hour. His head was decapitated and shown to the crowd; his heart was removed and burned; and his body was scored with a knife as a symbolic form of quartering. When David Tyrie was executed at Portsmouth on 24 August 1782, the sentence was carried out in full.

There was another hanging, drawing, and quartering at Maidstone on 7 July 1798. The victim was James O'Coigley who was executed for 'compassing and imagining the death of the king and adhering to the king's enemies'. He had conspired to foment a rising in Britain and Ireland that would coincide with a French invasion. It is not known how much of the sentence was actually carried out.

By the nineteenth century, although the same hideous sentence was still being passed, condemned traitors were at least hanged until pronounced dead. The corpse was beheaded and the grisly part of the sentence remitted. In 1802, one of O'Coigley's co-conspirators, Colonel Edward Despard, organized a new conspiracy to assassinate George III and start an uprising by taking over the Bank of England and the Tower of London. Despard was arrested along with six other accomplices. All were tried and found guilty of high treason even though Lord Nelson spoke in Despard's defence and the jury recommended mercy 'on account of his former services.' The full sentence was read out according to law, though by this time the part about castration had already been omitted. When the execution warrant arrived, it made no mention of disembowelling or quartering. Despard showed little gratitude for these small mercies. On the morning of 21 February 1803, after he had said goodbye to his wife and had his shackles removed, he refused the consolation of religion and, taking one look at the sled upon which he was going to be drawn cried: 'Ha! What nonsensical mummery is this?'

The seven men were to be executed on a gallows built on top of the Surrey County Gaol in Horsemonger Lane, Newington. One hundred invited guests packed the platform and the surrounding streets were filled with troops in case of insurrection. On the scaffold, Despard denied treason and claimed to be 'a friend to truth, to liberty, and to justice...to the poor and the oppressed'. The crowd of some 20,000 cheered. The seven men were hanged and left there for half an hour before being cut down and beheaded.

These were revolutionary times. On 7 November 1803, Jeremiah Brandreth, William Turner, and Isaac Ludlam, three of the leaders of the Pentrich Revolution, an armed insurrection against pay and conditions in the Nottingham area, were hanged and beheaded in Derby. The following day *The Times* reported:

'The executioner raised the axe and struck at the neck with all his force. At that instant there was a burst of horror from the crowd. The executioner then took up the head, and holding it by the hair, addressed the people: "Behold the head of Jeremiah Brandreth, the traitor." Hitherto the multitude had been quiet and motionless. The instant the head was exhibited, there was a tremendous shriek set up and they ran violently in all directions, as if under the impulse of a sudden frenzy. Those that resumed their stations groaned and hooted. The javelin-men and constables were all in motion, and a few dragoons, who had been stationed at both ends of the street, drew nearer with drawn swords. But all became immediately calm. Very few of the immense multitude now remained, and these looked quietly on while the heads of Turner and Ludlam were successively exhibited in the same way. The heads and bodies were then thrown into the coffins and all spectators dispersed.'

The Cato Street Conspiracy

The last men in England sentenced to be hanged, drawn, and quartered were Arthur Thistlewood, Richard Tidd, John Brunt, James Ings, and William Davidson. Collectively known as the Cato Street Conspirators, they were executed at the Old Bailey outside Newgate Prison on 1 May 1820. Like Despard, O'Coigley, and their cohorts, they had been inspired by the American and French revolutions and aimed to foment one in Britain, too. They planned to murder the Cabinet, kill the king, and rescue Napoleon from captivity on St Helena. They were arrested as they set out from their safe house in Cato Street, off Edgware Road, found guilty of treason, and sentenced accordingly.

Any mention of castration was removed from the sentence. Disembowelling and quartering were also remitted. The sheriff who

organized the execution also decided to dispense with the drawing on a hurdle which would have been impossible with so many spectators packing the streets. The Sunday papers announced that the execution would take place outside Newgate Prison on the following Monday and thousands flocked to reserve a place. Rails were erected around the surrounding streets to keep the crowds back and these were guarded by constables and troops who had to be brought in to maintain order. Window seats overlooking the scaffold fetched between ten shillings and two guineas (50p and £2.10 or £30 and £120 in today's money). Plans to build a new scaffold on the top of the prison were abandoned. Instead the ordinary scaffold used for hangings was extended to make room for decapitation and it was decked with black cloth and covered with sawdust to mop up the blood.

The author of the *Newgate Calendar*, who was behind the scenes that morning, reported the following:

'At seven o'clock, the crowd which was collected about the prison, in every avenue leading to it, or commanding the most distant glimpse of its walls, was beyond calculation; but still there was not the least appearance of disorder. In fact, such were the formidable preparations to preserve the peace that no possible alarm could exist. In the event of a riot, however, the Lord Mayor was prepared with large boards on poles, ready to be used should it become necessary to read the Riot Act. Shortly after seven o'clock, the executioner made his appearance at the drop and placed the steps by which he was to ascend to tie the sufferers to the fatal beam. The sawdust, which had been previously collected in two small heaps on the second scaffold, was now spread over the boards.'

After that, the coffins were brought out and filled with sawdust so the blood would not leak out through the joints.

'The awful moment was now approaching when the ill-fated men were to be removed to another world. Each of them conversed freely with the officers who had them in charge, and severally declared that moment to be the happiest of their lives.

'Thistlewood came out of the condemned cell first. He bowed to the sheriffs and the gentlemen present. He looked very pale, cast up his eyes, and said, "I appears fine." He displayed an uncommon firmness, and held out his hands for the assistant executioner to bind them. He observed to people near him that he never felt in better spirits in his life. He was attired in the same apparel he wore during the trial. The composure he exhibited was striking but there was nothing like bravado or carelessness. He now advanced to the block to have his irons knocked off and, while the turnkey was in the act, Tidd next made his appearance; he came out of the cell to the press yard with an air of complete gaiety. He smiled during the time he was being pinioned, and continued quite cheerful during the time his irons were knocked off. The moment his legs were free from their burden, he ran towards

Facing page: Dramatic illustration of the arrest of the Cato Street conspirators at their safe house, from Cassell's *History of England*

Thistlewood, who had taken a seat on the bench (placed in the yard for the purpose), and said, "Well, Mr Thistlewood, how do you do?" and they shook hands most heartily. Thistlewood said he was never better. Tidd conversed in the most gay and cheerful manner with the turnkey, while he was driving the rivets out of his irons, and composedly assisted the man in taking them off.

'Ings then came out of the cell and danced as he came down the steps along the yard. He was dressed in his usual clothes as a butcher, a rough pepper-and-salt coloured worsted jacket, and a dirty cap. During the time his hands were being tied, he became thoughtful, afterwards he seemed hurried and in great mental pain, but before his irons were knocked off, he began to laugh and shout, and afterwards took a seat by the side of his fellow sufferers.

'Brunt was then brought into the press yard; he was perfectly composed but looked round eagerly to see his wretched companions. He nodded to them, and then held out his hands to have them tied. He said nothing during the time he was being pinioned and having his irons taken off but afterwards he addressed Thistlewood, Tidd, and Ings. He told them to keep up their spirits and to one of his companions he said, "All will soon be well".

'Davidson was then brought out of his cell. He seemed a little affected at the sight of his companions but soon regained that composure which he had evinced during the trials. His lips moved but he did not betray much anxiety till his irons were knocked off. He then looked wildly at the Reverend Mr Cotton and appeared to be in prayer, very devoutly; the others declared they were about to die in peace with all mankind but that they had all made up their minds on religious matters and were determined to die Deists.

'When the awful ceremony of pinioning the culprits by the yeoman of the halter was concluded, they each shook hands, and most fervently exclaimed, "God bless you". The Reverend Mr Cotton then began to read the burial service, commencing at the words, "I am the resurrection and the life", etc. and, the arrangements being completed, the procession advanced through the dark passages of the gaol, led by the sheriffs and under-sheriffs. The Reverend Mr Cotton moved first. Thistlewood followed, with his eyes fixed as it were in abstract thought, and apparently lost to his situation. A vacant and unmeaning stare pervaded his countenance, which seemed unmoved by the devotions of the pious Ordinary. Tidd walked next, and although somewhat affected by his situation, his manner was collected, manly, and unaffectedly firm. Ings came next, and was laughing without reserve, and used every forced effort to subdue the better feelings of nature, which might remind him of his awful situation; his conduct was more like a delirium of fear than an effect of courage. Brunt, in fixed and hardened obduracy of mind, next advanced and, with a sullen and morose air of indifference, surveyed the officers who were conducting him to his fate. The unhappy Davidson came last, with his hands and uplifted eyes, praying most devoutly, and the officers of the gaol closed the mournful procession.

'On their arrival at the Lodge, from which the Debtors' Door leads to the *scaffold, a moment's pause took place while the dreadful paraphernalia of death were adjusted without. Thistlewood, who stood first, clasped his lips and with a frown surveyed from the doorway in which he stood the awful preparations for his fate. Those opposite the prison saw in the next moment the procession from the interior of it reach the door through which the culprits were to pass to expiate their crimes with their blood.*

'The Ordinary ascended the platform, and at a quarter before eight, Thistlewood made his appearance on the scaffold. His step faltered a little as he mounted the platform and his countenance was somewhat flushed and disordered on being conducted to the extremity of the drop. His deportment was firm, and he looked round at the multitude with perfect calmness. He had an orange in his hand. On the cap being placed on his head, he desired that it might not be placed over his eyes. While the executioner was putting the rope round his neck, a person from the top of the houses exclaimed, "God Almighty bless you". Thistlewood nodded. The Reverend Mr Cotton, by whom he was preceded, endeavoured to obtain his attention but he shook his head and said "No, no". He looked round repeatedly as [if] expecting to recognize someone in the crowd and appeared rather disconcerted at observing the distance to which the populace were removed.

'Some of those to whom the face of Thistlewood was not familiar imagined that he gave proofs of the fear of death upon the scaffold but in this supposition they were much mistaken. At the moment that he has been uttering his dangerous politics in safety, the expression of his features was the same and Thistlewood with the rope round his neck was the same Thistlewood that appeared so conspicuous at Smithfield.'

[Thistlewood had been one of the leaders of the Spa Field Riot in Smithfield in 1816.]

'Mr Cotton approached him while the executioner was making his awful arrangements and spoke to him upon the subject of his thoughts hereafter. Thistlewood shook his head, and said he required no earthly help on that subject. He then sucked his orange and, looking down at the officers, who were collected about the scaffold, said in a firm voice, "I have but a few moments to live, and I hope the world will be convinced that I have been sincere in my endeavours and that I die a friend to liberty".

'The figure of the miserable man, which naturally was not good, had undergone a change for the worse; in consequence of the pressure of the rope with which his arms were fastened behind, his shoulders were raised to a degree that closely approached deformity. The executioner, having placed the cap upon his head and fastened the rope round the beam, looked towards the sheriff as a signal that his duties towards Thistlewood were completed.

'While the executioner was performing his last offices without to this wretched man, the scene within the Lodge was almost beyond the power of description. The dreadful obduracy of Brunt and Ings filled with horror the small assemblage of persons among whom they stood. Ings, with a hardihood almost indescribable,

Facing page: The Cato
Street conspirators are
hanged and beheaded
outside Newgate Prison,
London, 1st May 1820, for
their part in the plot to kill
the entire British cabinet.
The castration part of the
sentence was ignored by
the authorities

sucked an orange and screamed in a discordant voice, "Give me death or liberty!"
Blunt rejoined, "Aye, to be sure. It is better to die free than to live as slaves."

'Tidd, who had stood in silence, was now summoned to the scaffold. He shook
hands with all but Davidson, who had separated himself from the rest. He ran
towards the stairs leading to the scaffold. In his hurry, his foot caught on the bottom
step and he stumbled. He recovered himself, however, in an instant and rushed
upon the scaffold, where he was immediately received with three cheers from the
crowd in which he made a slight effort to join. The rope having been put round his
neck, he told the executioner that the knot would be better on the right than on the
left side, and that the pain of dying might be diminished by the change. He then
assisted the executioner and turned round his head several times for the purpose of
fitting the rope to his neck. He also desired that the cap might not be put over his
eyes, but said nothing more. He likewise had an orange in his hand, which he
continued to suck most heartily. He soon became perfectly calm and remained so till
the last moment of his life.

'Ings followed and rushed to the platform, upon which he leaped and bounded
in the most frantic manner. Then, turning himself round towards Smithfield and
facing the very coffin that was soon to receive his mutilated body, he raised his
pinioned hands, in the best way he could, and leaning forward with savage energy,
roared out three distinct cheers to the people in a voice of the most frightful and
discordant hoarseness.

'Davidson walked up the platform with a firm and steady step but with all that
respectful humility becoming the condition to which he had reduced himself. He
bowed to the crowd and instantly joined Mr Cotton in prayer.

'Brunt was the last summoned to the fatal platform, and he rushed upon it with
impetuosity. Some of the people cheered him, which evidently gratified and pleased
him. It brought a sort of grin on his countenance, which remained until his death.
While the rope was being adjusted, he looked towards St Sepulchre's Church, and
perceiving or affecting to perceive someone with whom he had been acquainted, he
nodded several times and then made an inclination of his head towards the coffins
as if in derision of the awful display. His conduct was marked by the same
irrational levity to the last. His last act was to take a pinch of snuff from a paper
which he held in his hand. He also threw off his shoes.

'The executioner was now proceeding to adjust the ropes and to pull the caps
over the faces of the wretched men. When he came to Ings, the unhappy man said,
"Now, old gentleman, finish me tidily. Tie the handkerchief tight over my eyes. Pull
the rope tighter; it may slip." Tidd's lips were in motion just before he was turned
off as if in prayer. Davidson was in the most fervent prayer.

'The executioner, having completed the details of his awful duty, walked down
the ladder and left Mr Cotton alone upon the scaffold. The reverend gentleman,
standing closer to Davidson than to any of the rest, began to read those awful
sentences which have sounded last in the ears of so many unhappy men. Suddenly
the platform fell and the agonies of death were exhibited in the view of the crowd in

their most terrific force. Thistlewood struggled slightly for a few minutes. The struggles of Ings were great. The assistants of the executioner pulled his legs with all their might and even then the reluctance of the soul to part from its native seat was to be observed in the vehement efforts of every part of the body. However, in the course of five minutes, all was still.

'*Exactly half an hour after they had been turned off, the order was given to cut the bodies down. The executioner immediately ascended the scaffold and drew the legs of the sufferers up, and placed the dead men, who were still suspended, in the sitting position, with their feet towards Ludgate Hill. This being done, the trapdoor was again put up and the platform restored to its original state. The executioner proceeded to cut Thistlewood down and, with the aid of an assistant, lifted the body into the first coffin, laying it on the back and placing the neck on the edge of the block. The rope was then drawn from the neck and the cap removed from the face.*

'*The last convulsions of expiring life had thrown a purple hue over the countenance, which gave it a most ghastly and appalling appearance, but no violent distortion of features had taken place. An axe was placed on the scaffold but this was not used. When the rope had been removed, and the coast and waistcoat forced down so as to leave the neck exposed, a person wearing a black mask, which extended over his mouth, over which a coloured handkerchief was tied and his hat slouched down so as to conceal part of the mask, and attired in a blue jacket and dark grey trousers, mounted the scaffold with a small knife in his hand, similar to what is used by surgeons in amputation, and advancing to the coffin, proceeded to sever the head from the body.*

'*When the crowd perceived the knife applied to the throat of Thistlewood, they raised a shout in which exclamations of horror and reproach were mingled. The tumult seemed to disconcert the person in the mask for the moment but, upon the whole, he performed the operation with dexterity and, having handed the head to the assistant executioner, who waited to receive it, he immediately retired, pursued by the hootings of the mob.*

'*The assistant executioner, holding the head by the hair over the forehead, exhibited it from the side of the scaffold nearest Newgate Street. A person attended on the scaffold who dictated to the executioner what he was to say and he exclaimed with a loud voice, "This is the head of Arthur Thistlewood, the traitor!" A thrilling sensation was produced on the spectators by the display of this ghastly object and the hissings and hootings of part of the mob were vehemently renewed.*

'*The same ceremony was repeated in front of the scaffold and on the side nearest Ludgate Street. The head was then placed at the foot of the coffin while the body, before being lifted up to bring the neck on the block, was forced lower down and, this done, the head was again put in its proper place at the upper end of the coffin, which was left open.*

'*The block was then moved by the hangman and placed at the head of the second coffin, and the same ceremony was performed on Tidd. The execution lasted an hour and eight minutes. It was a quarter before eight when Thistlewood walked up the steps leading to the fatal platform and it wanted seven minutes to nine when the head of Brunt was placed in the coffin.*

'The person who wore the mask and who performed the ceremony of decapitation is said to be the same person who beheaded Despard and his associates. This, however, may be doubted, as from the quickness and spring of his motions, he seemed to be a young man. His mode of operation showed evidently that he was a surgeon. On performing his dreadful duty, the edge of the first knife was turned by the vertebrae of Thistlewood and two others became necessary to enable him to finish his heart-appalling task.

'At a late hour in the evening, the wives of the executed men were informed by the keeper of Newgate that the bodies of their husbands were buried. In the course of the afternoon, a channel had been dug alongside the subterraneous passage that leads to the cells and, about seven in the evening, after the coffins had been filled with quicklime, they were strongly screwed up, placed in a line with each other, strewed over with earth, and finally covered with stones, and of course no trace of their end remains for any future public observation. On this circumstance being communicated to their unhappy wives, they were entirely overcome with the poignancy of their feelings.'

The End of Hanging and Beheading

The last recorded instance of hanging and decapitation in Britain took place a few months later in Scotland. Twenty-two men were sentenced for high treason for their involvement in the uprising of 1820, an attempt to seize the Carron Ironworks near Falkirk with its munitions in an effort to obtain better working conditions, universal male suffrage, and a Scottish Parliament. The rebels were captured at the Battle of Bonnymuir. Their two leaders, Andrew Hardie and John Baird, went to the gallows at Stirling on 8 September. On the scaffold, Hardie told onlookers: 'I die a martyr to the cause of truth and injustice'. After hanging for half an hour, their bodies were dropped in coffins with their necks over the edge so they could be decapitated. Their heads were then shown to the crowd. This bloodthirsty ceremony was enough to satisfy the authorities: the remaining twenty conspirators were reprieved and transported to a penal colony in Australia. However, the sentence of hanging, drawing, and quartering remained on the statute books as the punishment for high treason until it was repealed by the Forfeiture Act of 1870.

Quartering on the Continent

On the Continent, victims were often quartered alive by attaching horses to their arms and legs. The horses were then driven in opposite directions. The sixth-century chronicler Gregory of Tours described how Queen Brunhilde

had her limbs tied to the tails of four horses that were then whipped until they pulled her apart. He also recorded that 200 Frankish women had been killed in this manner by the Germanic Thuringians.

On 14 May 1610, Henry IV of France was assassinated by the Catholic fanatic François Ravaillac. In an attempt to discover the names of his co-conspirators, Ravaillac was tortured using a method known as the *brodequin* (boot). His legs were encased from the foot up to the knee inside a piece of apparatus and wedges were driven in between the leg and the case, tearing the flesh, crushing the bone, and causing excruciating pain. Ravaillac eventually passed out and had to be revived with wine. He confessed his crime, claiming he had been tempted by the devil but insisted he had acted alone. Nevertheless he was going to die in a horrible manner.

At three o'clock on the afternoon of 27 May 1610, Ravaillac was brought from the prison wearing only his shirt: in one hand, attached to his wrist by a chain, he carried the knife he had used to stab the king; in the other, he held a lighted torch. He was then driven to a church by tumbril to do penance. The two clergymen who rode in the cart with him made further attempts to persuade him to divulge the names of his accomplices but to no avail. He was taken to the Place de Grève and according to an eyewitness:

'This was the following of his death, an example of terror made known to all the world, to convert all bloody minded traitors from the like enterprise. At first coming to the scaffold, he crossed himself directly over the breast, a sign that he did not live and die an obstinate Papist; whereupon he was bound by the executioners to an engine of wood and iron, made like a St Andrew's Cross, according to the fashion of his body, and then the hand with the knife chained to it, wherewith he slew the king, and half the arm, was put into an artificial furnace, then flaming with fire and brimstone, wherein the knife, his right hand, and half the arm adjoining to it, was in the most terrible manner consumed, yet nothing would he confess, but yelled out such horrible cries as if he had been a devil or some tormented soul in hell, "Oh God!" and often repeated, "Jesu Marie!" And surely, if hell's tortures might be felt on earth, it was approved in this man's punishment, and though he deserved ten times more, yet humane nature might force us to pity his distress.

'After this, with tongs and iron pincers, made extreme hot in the same furnace, the appointed executioners pinched and seared the dugs [nipples] of his breasts, the brawns [muscles] of his arms and thighs, the calves of his legs, and other fleshy parts of his body, cutting out loops of flesh, and burned them before his face. Afterwards, in the same wounds thus made, they poured scalded oil, rosen, pitch, and brimstone melted together; yet would he reveal nothing, but did it of himself by the instigation of the devil and the reason was because the king tolerated two religions in his kingdom...

'The executioners put upon his stomach a rundle of clay, very hard, with a hole in the midst, and into the same hole they poured molten lead, till it was filled, yet

Facing page: Henri IV of France is assassinated while driving in his coach by Catholic fanatic François Ravaillac, 14 May 1610

revealed he nothing, but cried out with most horrible roars, even like the dying man tormented in the brazen bull of the tyrant Phalaris.

'But now to come to the finishing up of his life, and so that the last torture might in severity equal the first, they caused four strong horses to be brought, to tear his body to pieces, and to separate his limbs into four quarters; where being made to pay his last punishment, he was questioned again to make known the truth, but he would not, and so died without speaking one word of God or remembering the danger of his soul.

'But so strongly was his flesh and joints knit together that for a long time these four horses could not dismember him, nor in any way tear one joint from the other, so that one of the horses fainted, the which a merchant of the city of Paris perceiving, put to one of his own, being a horse of exceeding great strength, yet notwithstanding for all this, the executioners were constrained to cut the flesh under his arms and thighs with a sharp razor, by which means his body was the easier torn to pieces.

'But when this was done, the rage of the people grew so violent that they snatched the dismembered corpse out of the executioners' hands; some beat it asunder on the ground, others cut it to pieces with knives, so that there was nothing left but bones, which were brought back to the place of execution from where it had been dismembered, and there burned to cinders, and the ashes scattered into the wind, as he was thought unworthy of earthly burial.

'His goods and chattels were also declared to be forfeited and confiscated to the king. And it was further ordained that the house in which he was born be pulled down to the ground, the owner thereof being previously indemnified, and that no other building shall ever thereafter be erected on the foundations thereof; and that within fifteen days, his father and mother, by sound of trumpet and public proclamation in the city of Angoulême, be banished out of the kingdom, and forbid ever to return under penalty of being hanged and strangled, without any further form of process of the law. The court also forbid his brothers, sisters, uncles, and others henceforth to bear the said name of Ravaillac, enjoining them to change it to some other, under the like penalties.'

Another chronicler recorded seeing a similarly gruesome sight, though with some disturbing sexual overtones. The man being led to the scaffold was first ordered to strip. He begged to be allowed to keep his undergarments on but, as there were a great many women present, the executioner insisted he remove these, too. The prisoner obeyed reluctantly as if this were the worst part of the punishment. The women let out a great roar of approval while the men hooted as the victim was particularly well-built.

With his arms and legs bound, a rope was put around his neck and he was hoisted aloft. He swung there for a long time, his life slowly ebbing away, as the surgeon in attendance kept an eye on him in case he died. When his eyes finally protruded from their sockets and his tongue was lolling out, he was cut down and laid on a wooden bench upon the scaffold and lashed down with strong ropes. The executioner cut the man's stomach open while his assistant removed the intestines. A brazier was brought in to fry the insides and the executioner's assistant forced the victim to watch by turning his head in that direction.

The condemned man was struggling and screaming for mercy. Women in particular seemed eager to join in the spectacle. Looking down from windows or craning their necks for a better view, they urged the executioner to excise the man's genitals from his body. As he held these aloft, they gave a great cheer while the men let out a mock groan. The organs were then thrown on the brazier.

The prisoner, who was spewing blood by now, was lowered to the ground. A horse was tied to each arm and leg, then each animal moved in a different direction until the man lay suspended between them. The horses were whipped and began to pull away but they strained for half an hour before the man's bones began to crack. When the two arms finally came off, the other horses galloped away, dragging the bloody limbs behind them.

The body was still twitching in the middle of the crowd. The executioner, the chronicler said, was then 'possessed of a little mercy'. He took out a knife, deftly opened the victim's chest, and pulled out the beating heart which 'appeared to move a little in his hand, like a fish caught from the stream, and breathed its last'. It was held aloft for the crowd to see before being thrown in the brazier. The rest of the body was displayed on spikes around the city.

Robert-François Damiens

In France, the most famous live quartering was that of Robert-François Damiens who tried to assassinate Louis XV. On 5 January 1757, he stabbed the king as he was getting into his coach at Versailles but the monarch was wearing a thick winter coat and only sustained a superficial wound. Damiens was arrested and imprisoned in the same cell as Ravaillac. The prisoner was kept strapped down with only his left hand free so he could feed himself. The court chief had precise orders to taste every dish himself in case Damiens' accomplices tried to spare him a painful death by sneaking in poison. It was thought that he was part of a Jesuit conspiracy to kill the king but, despite being tortured with red-hot tongs, Damiens revealed no details of any plot and it became clear he was mentally deranged. Even so, he was destined to suffer the same terrible fate as Ravaillac.

The executioner Jean-Baptiste Sanson did not enjoy such cruelty and, according to his great-grandson and family biographer Henri-Clement, 'became almost mad with grief when he heard that he had to dismember' the victim. Nevertheless he sent his son, the seventeen-year-old Charles-Henri, to buy four horses. Nearer the time of the execution, Jean-Baptiste fell ill and was paralyzed; his younger brother, Nicolas Gabriel Sanson, took his place.

After a scaffold had been erected in the Place de Grève, Sanson went to the prison where Damiens was being held. According to Henri-Clement Sanson, 'Damiens was brought forth: he was carried in a leather bag which was closed over his shoulders, and only allowed his head to appear. He was extracted from this kind of straitjacket and told to kneel.'

The sentence was read out:

'The court declares Robert-François Damiens duly convicted of the crime of lèse-majesté *divine and human, for the very wicked, very terrible, and very detestable parricide perpetrated on the king's person; and therefore condemns the said Damiens to pay for his crime in front of the main gate of the Church of Paris. He will be taken there in a tipcart naked and will hold a burning wax torch weighing two pounds. There, on his knees, he will say and declare that he had committed a very mean, very terrible, and very dreadful parricide, and that he had wounded the king on the right side, for which he repents and begs pardon of God, the king and justice. When this will be done, he will be taken in the same tipcart to the Place de Grève and put on a scaffold. Then his breasts, arms, thighs, and legs will be tortured. While holding the knife with which he committed the said parricide, his right hand will be burnt. On his tortured body parts, melted lead, boiling oil, burning pitch, melted wax, and sulphur will be thrown. Then four horses will pull him apart until he is dismembered. His limbs will be thrown on the stake and his ashes will be spread. All his belongings, furniture, housings, wherever they are, will be confiscated and given to the king. Before the execution, the said Damiens will be put to the* question ordinaire et extraordinaire *to tell the names of his accomplices.'*

Damiens' face was 'as yellow as wax'. He asked the soldiers who had accompanied Sanson to assist him in getting up, as his torture wounds had not yet healed. Sanson put his hand on Damiens' shoulder to comfort him. He was offered food and wine, but accepted only a glass of wine, which he was unable to drink anyway.

'He was affected by a kind of paroxysm which, during the first part of my professional career, I had many occasions to remark in the most courageous and stoical convicts, a violent contraction of the muscles of the neck which prevents the culprit from swallowing,' said Henri-Clement Sanson.

'Damiens was then removed to the torture chamber…The executioners came forward and the questionnaire of Parliament enclosed the prisoner's leg in the 'boot', pulling the cords more tightly than he usually did. The pain must have been insufferable for Damiens shrieked; his face became livid, he threw back his head, and nearly fainted away. The surgeons approached, felt his pulse, and declared that the fit was not serious. Damiens opened his eyes and asked for drink; a glass of water was offered to him but he begged for wine, saying in a broken voice that his energy was failing him. Charles-Henri Sanson helped him carry the glass to his lips. When he had

Left: King Louis XV of France, for whose attempted assassination Damiens was brutally executed

drunk, he heaved a deep sigh, closed his eyes, and murmured a prayer. Torture began again, and for two hours and a quarter, the unfortunate Damiens endured the most excruciating sufferings. At the eighth brodequin, *the surgeons said the sufferer could stand no more…yet Damiens had only endured a small part of the sufferings which were in store for him.'*

When Sanson did his research, he discovered that the methods of torture and the excruciating death outlined in the warrant had not been carried out for almost 150 years. He dug up the old archives and eventually found a description of Ravaillac's execution. Like his elder brother, Nicolas Gabriel Sanson felt ill at the thought of having to inflict such pain but he managed to find a torturer by the name of Soubise, a descendant of one of Ravaillac's executioners, who was an expert with the burning pincers and who 'continued to promise Damiens all the horrors outlined in the warrant'.

Charles-Henri Sanson and his assistants stayed with the prisoner while Nicolas Gabriel went to the Place de Grève to make sure that everything was ready for the execution. He discovered that a drunken Soubise had forgotten to buy the required lead, sulphur, wax, and rosin: he also discovered that the wood required for the fire to heat up the torture instruments was damp. The city's lieutenant reprimanded the executioner for this incompetence and sent for his nephew, Charles-Henri Sanson. He despatched his assistants and instructed them to buy everything Soubise had forgotten but the shopkeepers, who knew what the items were for, were reluctant to sell them anything until they were physically threatened.

The whole business took so long that when Damiens finally arrived he was asked to sit on the steps of the scaffold while everything was made ready. He was even taken on a tour of the town hall to kill time. Finally, he begged the magistrates to take care of his wife and children who knew nothing about his fate. Back at the scaffold,

> 'the chafing-dish on which the sulphur was being burnt with the hot coals filled the atmosphere with acrid vapour. Damiens coughed and, while the assistants were making him fast to the platform, he looked at his right hand with the same expression of sadness which had appeared on his face when looking at his legs after torture. His arm was tied to an iron bar so that the wrist should overreach the last board of the platform. Gabriel Sanson brought the chafing-dish. When the blue flame touched Damien's skin, he uttered a frightful shriek and tried to break his bonds. But when the first pang had shot through him, he raised his head and looked at the burning hand without manifesting his feelings otherwise than by grinding his teeth. The first part of the execution lasted three minutes.'

There were more problems in store.

> 'Charles-Henri Sanson saw the chafing-dish trembling in his uncle's hands. By his pallor, which was almost as deadly as the sufferer's, and the shudder which made his limbs shake, he perceived that he could not proceed with the burning with red-hot pinchers; and he offered one hundred livres to one of the valets if he would undertake the horrible task. The man, whose name was André Legris, accepted. The remainder of the execution was proceeded with; every clause of the atrocious sentence was literally carried out, and, when the four horses had dismembered the body, the remains of Damiens were thrown in a pile. It was then discovered that the victim's hair, which was brown when he was brought to the Grève, had turned white as snow.'

It should be noted that the English translator of Henri-Clement Sanson's family memoir suppressed most of the 'sickening details'. However, there are other accounts which relate that Legris happily plucked the red-hot pincers from the fire and tore at Damiens' chest and limbs, ignoring his victim's screams. He then poured molten lead, boiling pitch, hot wax, oil, and rosin into the wounds. All these brutalities were carried out before the execution proper had even begun.

The crowd was pushed back and Damiens was carried down from the scaffold and laid on the ground. Ropes were tied around his mutilated arms

and legs and he began to scream again. 'When the ropes were tied, four stout, young, and lively horses were whipped into action,' wrote an eyewitness. Unfortunately, they were not trained to work as a team and their efforts were uncoordinated:

'They continued their repeated efforts for more than an hour, without making any progress towards dismembering him other than stretching his joints to a great length. This was probably due to the fact that the horses were young and vigorous. Consequently they were too wilful and unruly to pull with a concerted effort. The physician and surgeon on hand told the commissioners that, unless the main sinews were cut, it would be difficult, if not impossible, to carry out the sentence of dismemberment.

'As it was late in the day, and it was desirable to get the execution over with before it got dark, this was done. The executioner cut the sinews with a sharp knife. Once these were cut, the horses began to pull once more and, after several pulls, a thigh and an arm were torn from the body. Damiens looked at the severed limbs. He was still conscious after the other thigh was pulled off nor did he die until the other arm was also torn off.

Above: The quartering of Robert-François Damiens, would-be assassin of Louis XV of France

Right: Renowned Italian lover Giacomo Casanova, who witnessed Damiens' execution in Paris. Casanova himself fell foul of the law in England: here he is escorted to Newgate Prison for debt

'Once there was no sign of life left in him, the torso and the severed limbs were thrown into a blazing wood fire that had already been prepared. This continued burning until seven in the morning. Then, in accordance with the death warrant, his ashes were scattered in the wind.'

According to Henri-Clement Sanson, 'the execution of Damiens produced so fearful an impression on Gabriel Sanson that he quit the office of executioner and gave it to his nephew in return for a yearly stipend of two thousand four hundred livres'.

The Venetian libertine Giacomo Casanova was in Paris at the time and paid 600 francs for a window overlooking the scaffold. He took four lady friends to view the execution and was appalled by what he saw. 'Damiens was the fanatic who had tried to kill Louis XV in the belief he was doing good,' he wrote in his memoirs. 'He had only just pierced the king's skin but that made no difference. The populace at his execution called him a monster spewed up from hell to assassinate "the best" of kings, who they believed they adored and who they had named *"Le Bien-Aimé"* [The Well-Beloved]. Yet it was these same people who massacred the whole royal family, all the noblemen of France, and all those who gave the nation the fair character that made it esteemed, loved, and even taken as a model by all other nations.'

By the time Louis XV died in 1774, he was universally despised. His son, Louis XVI, paid the price of this hatred with his head in 1792 as one of the victims of the French Revolution. 'I watched the dreadful scene for four hours,' reported Casanova, 'but was several times obliged to turn my face away and to close my ears as I heard his piercing shrieks, half his body having been torn away.'

While Casanova averted his gaze from the torture scene, he noticed that the women who were with him did not. So engrossed in the scene were they that Casanova noticed that his friend Count Edoardo Tiretta had raised the dress of 'Madame XXX' as she leant out of the window and now proceeded to have intercourse with her without the woman noticing. 'Determining neither to interrupt my friend's enterprise nor to embarrass Madame XXX, I took up a position behind my beloved' – who was Madame XXX's niece. 'The rustling of dresses went on for two whole hours.'

When the execution was over, Tiretta pretended nothing had happened but, embarrassed in front of her niece, Madame XXX affected that she had 'patiently put up with all the brute had done'. The following day, she complained to Casanova that Tiretta had insulted her in an 'unheard-of manner...For two whole hours yesterday at the execution of that monster Damiens, he took the strangest advantage of his position behind me'. She asked Casanova to send for Tiretta so she could chastise him. By morning, she had forgiven him.

A Would-be Regicide

It was not just the French who treated would-be regicides in this barbarous way. The thirteenth-century English chronicler Matthew Paris recorded that:

'in 1238, Henry III was at Woodstock when a learned squire came to court. He feigned insanity and insisted that the king give up his crown. The courtiers tried to drive him away but the king said he should stay. That night the man returned with a knife and made his way to the king's chamber. But the king was not there; he was with the queen. One of the queen's maids named Margaret Bisseth, a holy maid and a devout servant of God, was awake. She raised the alarm and the man was arrested. The assailant admitted that he had come to kill the king. On hearing this, Henry ruled that anyone who tried to take the king's life should be torn limb from limb by horses as a terrible example; the horrible spectacle should deter anyone else from plotting such a crime. The man was torn apart by horses, then beheaded. His body was divided into three parts. Each was dragged through one of England's great cities. His remains were then hung on a thieves' gibbet.'

C H A P T E R   6

Burning

The Bible is full of references to burning as a form of righteous punishment. Consider Genesis, Chapter 38, Verse 24, 'Tamar, thy daughter-in-law, hath played the harlot; and moreover, behold, she is with child by whoredom. And Judah said, Bring her forth, and let her be burned', or John, Chapter 15, Verse 6, 'If a man abide not in me, he is cast forth as a branch, and is withered; and men gather them and cast them into the fire, and they are burned'.

Facing page: The Spanish Inquisition: burning 'witches' at the *auto-da-fé,* a regular occurence during Tomas de Torquemada's supremacy of that infamous organization

Christian Martyrs in Rome's Arenas

This terrible death was also inflicted on Christian martyrs. In his *History of the Martyrs of Palestine,* the fourth-century writer Eusebius of Caesarea records the terrible death handed out by the Emperor Maximinus to Apphianus. His feet were first wrapped in cotton that was soaked with oil, then set on fire:

'The martyr was hung up at a great height, in order than, by this dreadful spectacle, he might strike terror into all those who were looking on, while at the same time they tore his sides and ribs with combs, till he became one mass of swelling all over, and the appearance of his countenance was completely changed. And, for a long time, his feet were burning in a sharp fire, so that the flesh of his feet, as it was consumed, dropped like melted wax, and the fire burst into his very bones like dry reeds'.

Constantine, the Roman emperor who banned crucifixion, decreed that any slave who had had intercourse with a free woman should be burned alive. Not surprisingly, burning was the punishment for sexual misconduct most often prescribed in the Old Testament. Leviticus, Chapter 21, Verse 9 announced that if 'the daughter of any priest…profane herself by playing the whore, she profaneth her father: she shall be burnt with fire'. Leviticus, Chapter 20, Verse 14, declared that 'if a man take a wife and her mother, it is wickedness; they shall be burned with fire, both he and they; that they be no wickedness among you'.

The Spanish Inquisition

Burning became the Church's punishment of choice for heresy because it was not allowed to spill blood. Established by Pope Gregory IX in 1231, the Inquisition mainly conducted its barbarous business in northern Italy and southern France. A separate organization bearing the same name was set up in Spain by Pope Sixtus IV at the request of Ferdinand and Isabella, rulers of Aragon and Castile, after the expulsion of the Moors.

However, at the time that the Moors were being driven out of the Iberian peninsula, the political authorities in Aragon and Castile were also looking for a way to impose their authority on the rest of the country, so they persuaded Pope Sixtus IV to authorize a separate Spanish Inquisition in 1478. Its first *auto-da-fé* took place in Seville in 1481: hundreds were burned alive and the proceedings that were reported seemed so savage that the pope himself belatedly tried to ban it, to no avail. The king and queen found the Spanish Inquisition to be such a powerful political tool that they restored it, appointing their own Inquisitor-General, the Dominican Tomás de Torquemada. In his fifteen-year career as head of the Inquisition, he was personally responsible for burning more than 2,000 people at the stake.

Arrests usually took place at night. *Alguazils* (familiars of the Inquisition)

would knock on doors and force their way in if there was any resistance. The victim would be told to get dressed as he or she would be taken away immediately. The *alguazils* liked to work in silence: they brought a painful metal gag with them for anyone tempted to alert their neighbours by crying out. Non-Christians – such as Jews and Muslims – were in particular danger but so were recent converts.

Victims were brought to the Holy Office where every detail was designed to intimidate the suspect. The so-called 'trial' was held in a darkened room. The inquisitors, dressed in black-hooded white habits, were seated at a table swathed in black velvet, upon which were arranged a crucifix, a Bible, and six candles. If the victim failed to confess, he would be 'put to the question' (tortured). In the end, everyone either confessed or died in the torture chamber.

The Church could, on occasion, be merciful: individuals found guilty of heresy who asked to be reconciled with the Church were sometimes spared. Their penance was to be whipped half-naked through the city streets on six successive Fridays in a procession up to the local cathedral. They were forbidden from holding any rank or office and could not wear fine clothes or jewellery. One-fifth of their wealth was forfeited to the Church as a form of one-off 'penance tax'. These individuals could consider themselves fortunate: unreconciled heretics – those who relapsed or those not favoured by the Inquisition – suffered public burning at the *auto-da-fé*.

The *Auto-da-fé*

Auto-da-fé translates as 'act of faith' in Portuguese. The Spanish equivalent was *auto-de-fé* but, for historic reasons, the Portuguese variant would be adopted by the English language. These ghastly rituals were reserved for Sundays and other holy days when larger crowds were able to attend. Heretics were rounded up on the evening before the *auto* and brought before the Inquisition panel who passed judgement on them. Each condemned person would be allotted two priests, who would wrestle for their soul. Although the condemned were doomed, it was still considered desirable for the Church to save their souls from eternal damnation. If, during their last moments, they were seen to be reconciled with God, they would be spared the final agony and strangled before the flames reached them.

Every individual accused of heresy had to wear a *coraza*, a tall mitre-like cap, and a *sanbenito*, a loose-fitting, knee-length tunic made of yellow sackcloth regularly worn by penitents. Those found guilty of lesser crimes would be sentenced to wear the *sanbenito* on Sundays for a prescribed length of time as a penance. Normally, these tunics would have had blood-red crosses embroidered on them but those worn at the *auto-da-fé* were decorated in the best Grand Guignol tradition with flames and pitchfork-wielding

Facing page: An *auto-da-fé* at Goa, India – the procession of clergy and their victims, 20 of whom will shortly be burnt alive to save their souls

Above: As a prelude to burning a heretic alive, the Inquisition would first make them confess their heresy

devils. If the flames pointed downwards, the Inquisition had been merciful: the victim had repented and would be strangled. If the flames pointed upwards, the victim was stubbornly persisting in his or her heretical beliefs and would suffer the worst agony – being burned alive.

At around six o'clock the next morning, the accused were lined up outside the prison in their *sanbenitos*, with a rope around their necks and their hands bound together. Priests bearing green crosses (the symbol of the Inquisition) draped in black cloth led the procession followed by the *alguazils*. As well as arresting suspects and visiting sinners in jail, in order to urge them to repent, these men acted as the bodyguards of the inquisitors who were not always popular figures in the community. Next came a priest carrying the holy Host in a monstrance. Over his head was a canopy of scarlet and gold carried by four men. When he approached, the men, women, and children in the crowd had to fall to their knees. If they did not do this, they would be singled out as heretics.

More *alguazils* followed in his wake and then lesser criminals, some of whom bore the marks of torture. Condemned heretics were flanked on either side by a Dominican friar in a white vestment and black hood, often still trying to save the soul of a victim as the procession moved on. There followed the corpses of those posthumously found guilty of heresy and exhumed as a punishment. Behind them came the effigies of those who had fled Spain rather than face the Inquisition; these statues were carried on green poles and wore the *corazas* and *sanbenitos* of the condemned.

Following the figures came the inquisitors, flanked on one side by banners emblazoned with the arms of the pope entwined with those of Ferdinand and Isabella, and on the other side by the arms of the Inquisition. Behind them followed more *alguazils* and other minor officials. The entire procession was protected by soldiers carrying halberds and bringing up the rear was the crowd who accompanied the cortège up to the cathedral in the main square.

A list of crimes was read out to each victim, followed by the delivery of a blood curdling sermon. Often there were several hundred victims to be tried – who were seated on benches swathed in black crepe – and it could take all

Left: Tomás de Torquemada, ascetic monk, head of the Spanish Inquisition and enthusiastic interrogator of anyone suspected of heresy

Right: The *auto-da-fé* in full swing. The condemned, dressed in brightly-coloured *sanbenitos*, are led to the *quemadero*, the place of burning

day. These benches were set along the platform so the crowd could see the condemned clearly. It was not unusual, for example, to set fire to the beards of Jews, a form of humiliation known as 'shaving the New Christians'. All the while, victims continued to be harried by priests and monks still working hard to extract last-minute confessions.

The inquisitors sat on another platform surrounded by their green, black-draped crosses. Incense was burnt as a wise precautionary measure because

there was usually a fairly large number of freshly disinterred bodies lying around. Mass was celebrated and another sermon delivered before the Grand Inquisitor stood up and led the crowd in a pledge. Onlookers were required to fall to their knees and swear an oath that they would defend the Holy Office against its enemies, remain faithful to it in life and in death and do whatever it asked of them, even if that meant plucking out an eye or cutting off a hand.

Ferdinand and Isabella refrained from uttering this oath as did the Spanish monarchs who succeeded them. The only exception was the eccentric Philip II who was a zealot. After the oath, the Church would wash its hands of the sinners; in its eyes, it had done all it could for them. The clergy abandoned the prisoners to the secular authorities for the punishment for heresy to be carried out. The charges were read out again, this time by the civil authorities. The Grand Inquisitor made a public plea for mercy disingenuously requesting that blood should not be spilt.

The secular authorities were, of course, deaf to these false pleas. They took the victims to the *quemadero* or place of burning, usually an open field where stakes had been set up and firewood piled high. Victims were tied to the stake and asked whether they wanted an absolution: the lucky ones were garrotted before the faggots were lit. The monks chanted and the people cheered whilst the inquisitors feigned shock at the wickedness of the world. The smell of roasting flesh filled the air.

After perfecting such cold-blooded ritual, and murdering thousands of innocents, Torquemada died peacefully in his bed in 1498, a happy man. He had lived to see the Muslims expelled from Granada and his own persecution had resulted in the expulsion of the Jews in 1492. At the time many people called him the 'Saviour of Spain' because he had freed the country from papal control. It is now shocking to think that many of the subsequent grand inquisitors were even more wicked.

At the height of its power, the Spanish Inquisition boasted fourteen tribunals in Spain, Mexico, and Peru. It also established satellites in Sicily in 1517 but efforts to set up in Naples and Milan backfired. In 1522, Emperor Charles V introduced this institution to the Netherlands in an effort to stamp out Protestantism and Napoleon attempted to suppress it in 1808 when he occupied Spain. The Inquisition was finally brought to an end in 1834 and the last *auto-da-fé* took place in Mexico in 1850. Estimates of the number of victims of the Inquisition vary considerably, but they probably ran into the hundreds of thousands. What is known, however, is that the majority were women, some of them very elderly. Children as young as twelve or thirteen frequently burned when their parents were found to be heretics. In 1659, two ten-year-old girls were consumed by flames in Toledo.

As well as punishing 'wrong-doers', public burnings served to intimidate onlookers. An eyewitness to a burning in the Middle Ages described the spectacle thus:

'You could see the white bones showing through as the skin and flesh of the man slowly dragged itself away from the skeleton and fell, in a pink and orange and red-raw curtain, down towards his feet, which were festooned with flames. The face, too, gradually, seemed to leave the skull and jawbone by degrees, the chin sagging down, the mouth following with all sorts of wry grimaces, and dropping away with the

nose suddenly elongated and slithering and sliming itself away down the teeth, which showed through the moving film of flesh. The forehead followed, after the eyeballs appeared to be spilled out from their sockets, liquid and white, and green, blue, and brown, according to the person's colouring. Last comes the crown of the head, molten and turgid, revealing white skull beneath gently smouldering hair. Soon all that remained were bones, charred and blackened, and bits of obstinate, purple flesh that persists in hanging on the bones. Thousands of spectators watched these burnings and it could take three-quarters of an hour to die'.

Burning English Heretics

The English also burned heretics and apostates. In 1222 in Oxford, for example, a Christian deacon was condemned for converting to Judaism in order to marry a Jewish woman. At that time, men who lived with female Jews were regularly sentenced to death for having 'committed an unnatural offence'. In 1401, Henry IV signed the Statute of Heresy giving the clergy powers to arrest those they believed were spreading heresy. Those who recanted were merely jailed; those who did not were burned at the stake. The first to suffer this appalling punishment was a priest called William Sautre at St Paul's Cross, Lynn, in March 1402.

Henry VIII had a macabre talent for inventing similarly hideous deaths. Although he executed over 72,000 people – an average of more than five people daily – during the course of his 38-year reign, he wanted a particularly gruesome end to befall Richard Roose. This man had been convicted of putting poison in a pot of broth intended for the family of the Bishop of Rochester and the poor of the parish.

King Henry passed a special act in 1530 decreeing that Roose was to be boiled alive. Margaret Davey suffered the same terrible fate in 1542 at Smithfield. It also became customary for executioners to use a huge frying pan with a handle, where a prisoner's body could be turned like a piece of meat. Death did not come quickly in either case if the victim's heart was strong. Much of the flesh could be cooked from the bone before the heart, lungs, and brain felt the effects of heat.

Henry's son, Edward VI, was horrified by these barbaric practices and passed a law downgrading wilful poisoning to the regular felony of murder punishable by hanging. Only women who had tried to poison their husbands or children would be burned. His father's original act, however, remained in the statute book until 1863.

Although Henry VIII was considered a heretic, he was happy to condemn others on religious grounds. Following his breach with Rome, he repealed the Statute of Heresy in 1533 but signed the Religion Act of 1542 which banned the Bible and any other religious work that had been translated into English. The act also declared that 'no person shall play in enterlude, sing,

Right: Holbein's portrait of Henry VIII captures something of the king's strength of character, but also his petulance

or rhime, contrary to the said doctrine'. The punishment for a first offence was to recant, 'for his second to abjure and bear a faggot, and for his third shall be adjudged an heretic and be burned and lose all his goods and chattels'. To 'bear a faggot' meant being burned at the stake but at least no property was forfeited. The act was repealed after Henry's death in 1547.

'Bloody Mary'

Henry VIII's Catholic daughter, Mary I, burned over 274 Protestants as heretics, largely in the Smithfield area. Although she has gone down in history with the nickname of 'Bloody Mary', she was more merciful than most, allowing those sentenced to the stake to carry gunpowder on their person in the hope of a speedy demise. It did not always work. In 1555, Dr John Hooper, Bishop of Gloucester, was burned at the stake in front of 7,000 spectators. The event is described at length in Henry Moore's *The History of the Persecutions of the Church of Rome and Complete Protestant Martyrology* :

'The place of execution was near a great elm tree, over against the college of priests, where he used to preach; the spot round about and the boughs of the trees was filled with spectators. Bishop Hooper then knelt down and prayed. Having closed his devotional exercises, the bishop prepared himself for the stake. He took off his doublet, hose, and waistcoat. Being now in his shirt, he trussed it between his legs, where he had a pound of gunpowder in a bladder, and under each arm the same quantity. He now went up to the stake, where three iron hoops were brought, one to fasten him round the waist, another round the neck, and another his legs; but he refused to be bound with them, saying, "You have no need to trouble yourselves; I doubt not God will give me strength sufficient to abide the extremity of the fire without bands; notwithstanding, suspecting the frailty and weakness of the flesh, but having assured

Left: Mary I of England's reputation for the persecution of Protestants earned her the sobriquet 'Bloody Mary'

confidence in God's strength, I am content you do as you think good". The iron hoop was then put round his waist, which being made too short, he shrank and put in his belly with his hand; but when they offered to bind his neck and legs, he refused saying, "I am well assured I shall not trouble you". Being affixed to the stake, he lifted up his eyes and hands to Heaven, and prayed in silence. The man appointed to kindle the fire then came to him and requested his forgiveness, of whom he asked why he should forgive him, since he knew of no offence he had committed against him. "O sir (said the man), I am appointed to make the fire." "Therein," said Bishop Hooper, "thou dost nothing to offend me: God forgive thee thy sins, and do thy office I pray thee." Then the reeds were thrown up, and he received two bundles of them in his own hands, and put one under each arm. Command was now given that the fire should be kindled; but, owing to the number of green faggots, it was some time before the flames set fire to the reeds. The wind being adverse, and the morning very cold, the flames blew from him, so he was scarcely touched by the fire. Another fire was soon kindled of a more vehement nature: it was now the bladders of gunpowder exploded, but they proves of no service to the suffering prelate. He now prayed with a loud voice, "Lord Jesus, have mercy upon me; Lord Jesus, have mercy upon me; Lord Jesus, receive my spirit" and these were the last words he was heard to utter. But even when his face was completely black with the flames and his tongue swelled so that he could not speak, yet his lips went until they shrank to the gums; and he knocked his breast with his hands until one of his arms fell off, and then continued knocking with the other while the fat, water, and blood dripped out at his finger ends. At length, by renewing of the fire, his strength was gone, and his hand fastened in the iron which was put round him. Soon after, the whole lower part of his body being consumed, he fell over the iron that bound him, into the fire, amidst the horrible yells and acclamations of the bloody crew that surrounded him. This holy martyr was more than three quarters of an hour consuming; the inexpressible anguish of which he endured as a lamb, moving neither forwards, backwards, nor to any side: his nether parts were consumed, and his bowels fell out some time before he expired. Thus perished, in a manner the most horrible that the rage of hell itself could devise, in a manner more barbarous than exercised by wild American Indians to their prisoners taken in war, the right reverend father in God, Dr John Hooper, for some time the Bishop of Worcester and afterwards Gloucester.'

According to Moore's *Martyrology*, Hooper got off lightly. That year the Reverend George Marsh was also burned. 'The fire,' said Moore, 'being unskilfully made, and the wind contrary, he suffered extreme torture'. Moore had called burning a practice 'more barbarous than exercised by wild American Indians to their prisoners taken in war'. In fact, it was a method of execution that the Europeans themselves had exported to the New World. Bartolomé De Las Casas, the sixteenth-century missionary who first exposed Spanish brutality in the Americas, wrote the following: 'I once beheld four or five principal Indians roasted alive at a slow fire, and as the miserable victims

Lord Jesus receive my Soul

Above: Dr John Hooper, Bishop of Gloucester, burnt at the stake for heresy in 1655

poured forth dreadful screams, which disturbed the commanding officer in his afternoon slumbers, he sent word that they should be strangled but the officer on guard (I know his name, and I know his relations in Seville) would not suffer it; but causing their mouths to be gagged, that their cries might not be heard, he stirred up the fire with his own hands, and roasted them deliberately till they all expired – I saw it myself'.

The Oxford Martyrs

Perhaps the most famous of Protestant martyrs under Mary were Bishops Hugh Latimer and Nicholas Ridley. Under Henry VIII, Latimer had twice been imprisoned for his preaching, but returned to favour under Edward. With the ascencion of Mary to the throne, however, he once more found himself on the wrong side of a monarch. Condemned as a heretic, Latimer was sentenced to be burnt outside Balliol College, Oxford on 16 October, 1555. With him was his friend and fellow-Protestant Bishop Nicholas Ridley, who in 1530 was instrumental in the Cambridge University declaration that 'the Bishop of Rome had no more authority and jurisdiction derived to him from God, in this kingdom of England, than any other foreign bishop.' The declaration did not sit well with the avidly Catholic Mary.

Both men died bravely, although Ridley died very hard, as the flames took some time to consume him. Latimer's last words have found a particular resonance in history: 'Play the man, Master Ridley; we shall this day light such a candle, by God's grace, in England, as I trust shall never be put out.'

The Martyrdom of Dr. Ridley an...

Right: The deaths of Bishops Ridley and Latimer ensured their martyrdom for centuries to come

The last man to be burned to death in England was the Baptist minister Edward Wightman, who perished in 1612 for denouncing infant baptism as practised by the Church of England. Incredibly, he faced the flames twice. On the first occcasion, he recanted when the fire reached him and he was pulled out by spectators, some of whom were badly injured in the process. Once back in prison, he had second thoughts and refused to sign a formal recantation. A month later, he went to the stake again and this time his retractions were ignored.

Women were burned for high treason instead of being hanged, drawn, and quartered. The great jurist Sir William Blackstone explained: 'for as

T. Latimer at OXFORD.

decency due to their sex forbids the exposing and public mangling of their bodies, their sentence is to be drawn to the gallows and there to be burnt alive'. During the time of Mary I, however, women would die naked, although they were permitted a bag filled with gunpowder around the neck to hasten death.

Among his catalogue of inhumane punishments, Judge Jefferys sentenced Lady Alice Lisle to burning alive, for her part in protecting participants in the failed Monmouth uprising of 1685. After the clergy stepped in to plead for mercy, however, clemency was granted and she was beheaded instead.

Petty Treason

'Coining' (coin forgery) was considered treason as it usurped the sovereign's privilege to make currency. It was for this offence that Barbara Spencer was sentenced to the stake at Tyburn in 1721. According to the *Newgate Calendar*:

'When she stood at the stake she seemed to have less fear than on the preceding day. She was very desirous of praying and complained of the dirt and stones thrown by the mob behind her, which prevented her thinking sedately on futurity. One time she was quite beat down by them. She declared that she had been taught to coin by a man and a woman who had now left it off, and lived reputably, though when they first began that trade, they were in very poor circumstances; but she would not discover who they were, it being, in her opinion, a pity that a family should be ruined who had given over that practice, and so many hundreds live secure in London who still continue the same; and added that, though she saw the faggots lie ready to burn her, she would never take away the life of another by making herself an evidence, even if a magistrate was to come in person and offer her a pardon to do it. And therefore she found it difficult to forgive Miles, her old companion and accuser. But, however, just before the fire was kindled, she forgave not only her, but all the world, and died in perfect charity'.

Barbara Spencer was strangled before the flames got to her. However, other individuals were not so lucky. Women were also be burned for 'petty treason' – that is, murdering their husbands or masters – and husband-murderer Catherine Hayes was burned alive at Tyburn in 1726. 'On the day of her death,' reported the *Newgate Calendar*:

'Hayes received the Sacrament and was dragged on a sledge to the place appointed for her execution. When the wretched woman had finished her devotions, in pursuance of her sentence, an iron chain was put around her waist, with which she was attached to the stake. When women were burned for petty treason, it was usual to strangle them by means of a rope passed around the neck and pulled by the executioner, so that they were mercifully insensible to the heat of the flames. But this

woman literally burnt alive, for the executioner let go of the rope too soon in consequence of having his hand burnt by the flames. The flames burned fiercely around her, and the spectators beheld Catherine Hayes pushing away the faggots while she rent the air with cries and lamentations. Other faggots were instantly piled on her but she survived amidst the flames for a considerable time and her body was not perfectly reduced to ashes until three hours later'.

Above: Although it was customary for the executioner to strangle the victims of burning first, sometimes this was not entirely effective, as in the case of Catherine Hayes

The last burning at Newgate took place on 18 March 1789. Christine Murphy and her husband were sentenced to death for the offence known as coining. He was one of eight men hanged in front of Newgate gaol that morning. She was brought out soon after and chained to a stake a few yards from the scaffold before being hanged from the wooden arm that projected from the top of the stake. The unfortunate woman was left to swing for half an hour before firewood was piled around her body and set alight. Burning as a form of punishment was formally abolished in 1790.

Around the World

Burnings also took place in colonial America. In 1741, twenty-nine blacks and four whites were sentenced to death for conspiring to burn down the city of New York. Twenty-two people were hanged in total: eighteen blacks, two white men, and two white women. The other eleven offenders burned at the stake. The last case of this kind was reported in Abbeville County, South Carolina, in 1825. A slave named Negro Jack was convicted of rape and murder by the magistrates of an inferior court and by five freeholders and sentenced to the stake. The conviction was deemed so untenable that South Carolina later repealed any law that permitted execution by burning.

The Japanese practised a particularly unpleasant variation on burning where they would hang a victim upside down by his feet, with his head inside a pit. The fire would be built on a platform that enclosed the person's neck. In this way, the head was left intact as the body burned away, prolonging the agony for as long as possible.

The Germans also punished specific offences by burning. The executioner of Nuremberg, Franz Schmidt, recorded in his notebook on 13 August 1594: 'Christopher Meyer, a weaver of fustian, and Hans Weber, a fruiterer, both citizens of this town, who for three years practised sodomy together and were informed against by a hookmaker's apprentice who caught them in the act behind a hedge. The fruiterer had practised buggery for twenty years, that is with the cook Endressen, with Alexander, and others. The weaver was first beheaded, then his body was burnt with the fruiterer, who was burnt alive'.

In Scotland, crimes of bestiality attracted the penalty of death by fire. On 17 September 1605, Johnne Jak (alias Scott) was consumed by flames along with a mare believed to have been his partner in crime. Witches were also sentenced thus in Scotland and the Channel Islands but rarely in England and America where they were usually hanged. The Scottish authorities made convicted witches even pay for their punishment. When Janet Wishart and Isabel Crocker were condemned in February 1596, they were presented with an itemized bill for the various expenses associated with the burnings (the total bill came to £11 10s):

	Shillings	pence
For twenty loads of peat to burn the victims	40	0
For a boll [six bushels] of coal	24	0
For four tar barrels	26	3
For fir and iron barrels	16	8
For a stake and the dressing of it	16	0
For four fathoms [24 feet] to tows [hangman's rope]	4	0
For carrying the peat, coals, and barrels up the hill	8	4
One justice for their execution	13	4

On 19 November 1636, William Coke and his wife, Alison Dick, were accused and sentenced for witchcraft at Kirkcaldy. To help them burn, they were dressed in hemp garments specially made for the occasion and then placed in barrels of tar. They were too poor to pay up so the kirk and the town council received this bill:

	£	s	d
For ten loads of coal to burn them five marks	3	6	8
For tows		14	0
For hurden [hemp fabric] and jumps [short coats]	3	10	0
For making the garments		8	0
For one to go to Finmouth for the laird to sit upon their assize as judge		6	0
For the executioner for his pains	8	14	0
For his expenses here		16	0

Public burning was also practised in France. When the last stronghold of the Cathar sect – the fortress of Montségur in the Pyrenees (whose treasures were thought to include the Holy Grail) – fell in March 1244, after a ten-month-long siege, 200 men and women walked out of the fortress singing and straight into the funeral pyres prepared for them by the crusaders.

When the Templars – another sect – were suppressed in 1307, many of their knights were burned at the stake, including the order's last grand master, Jacques De Molay, whereupon an obsession with witchcraft seemed to seize hold of France. By 1350, the inquisitions at Toulouse and Carcassonne had prosecuted 1,000 people for witchcraft and 600 of these had died by fire. In 1431, Joan of Arc was charged with witchcraft and heresy, and burned in public, although the motivation for her conviction was more political than theological in nature.

Right: Jacques de Molay, last grand master of the Templars, is burned in Paris, 1307. The Templars' fate set the tone for the great French witch persecutions

Although the story of Joan of Arc is familiar to most people, it is perhaps less well known that Joan was actually executed for heresy, rather than witchcraft. Inspired by her 'visions', the simple peasant girl had led the French armies to several victories against the Burgundians and the English, including raising the siege of Orleans in May 1429. Joan had also been instrumental in forcing the kingship claim of Charles VII to the French throne: he was crowned in Rheims on 17 July, 1429. Joan eventually fell into the hands of her enemies at Compiégne, apparently due to her insistence on being the last to leave the field of battle. Sold to the English by the Burgundians, Joan could have been ransomed by Charles VII, the king she had helped to crown, but for reasons of his own Charles chose to ignore his erstwhile commander.

Joan's trial for heresy was presided over by Pierre Cauchon, the Bishop of Beauvais, a man with his eye on the archbishopric, and a keen appreciation of English power within France. Convicted of heresy, Joan had her sentence commuted to life imprisonment, rather than the stake when she recanted her belief in her visions, and also agreed to revert to wearing women's clothes, rather than the male garb in which she had waged war.

When she resumed wearing men's clothes shortly after her trial, however, this was seen as the act of an unrepentant heretic, and Joan was condemned to be burnt, officially for heresy, but in actuality the victim of an ambitious cleric.

Throughout the fifteenth and sixteenth centuries, the French continued to punish anyone suspected of being either a witch or a werewolf. In 1633, the nuns of the small Ursuline convent at Loudun accused the local parish priest, Father Urbain Grandier, of sorcery. A handsome man with an eye for the ladies, he made no secret of the fact that one of his young penitents was also his mistress. When another girl became pregnant, he was charged with immorality but his actual crime was the publication of a satire against Cardinal Richelieu. When the nuns appeared to show signs of demonic possession, a cohort of Richelieu's was sent in to investigate the matter. The nuns claimed Grandier had sent demons to torment them, spurned mistresses spoke out against him, and a written document purporting to be a pact drawn up between Grandier and Lucifer himself was promptly produced.

On 18 August 1634, the following judgement was handed down:

'We have ordered and do order the said Father Urbain Grandier, duly tried and convicted of the crime of magic, maleficia, *and of causing the demonic possession of several Ursuline nuns of this town of Loudun, as well as of other secular women, together with other charges and crimes resulting therefrom. For atonement of which, we have condemned and do condemn the said Grandier to make amends publicly, his head bare, a rope around his neck, holding in his hand a burning candle*

weighing two pounds, before the main door of the church of St-Pierre-du-Marché, and before that of St Ursula of this town. There on his knees to ask pardon of God, the king, and the law. This done, he is to be taken to the public square of St Croix and fastened to a stake on a scaffold, which shall be erected on the said place for this purpose, and there to be burned alive, together with all the compacts and

Right: Joan of Arc, burnt in 1431. Ostensibly a heretic, Joan more immediately was a thorn in the side of the French king, Charles VII

magical apparatus used by him, as well as a manuscript of a book composed by him against the celibacy of priests and his ashes scattered to the wind. We have ordered and do order that each and every article of his moveable property be acquired and confiscated by the king; the sum of 500 livres, first being taken for buying a bronze plaque on which will be engraved the abstract of this present trial, to be set up in a prominent spot in the said church of the Ursulines, to remain there for all eternity. And before proceeding to the execution of the present sentence, we order the said Grandier to be submitted to the first and last degrees of torture, concerning his accomplices. Given at Loudun against the said Grandier and executed this day 18 August 1634'.

Grandier was tortured so severely that the marrow of his bones oozed out of his broken limbs but he pleaded his innocence throughout his ordeal and would name no accomplices. The priests who had accused him assisted in the torture and, enraged by his fortitude, smashed his legs. His silence, they asserted, proved his guilt. When he prayed to God, they said, he was actually invoking the devil.

The civil authorities took pity on Grandier. He was given permission to make a statement from the scaffold and strangled before his body was thrown to the flames. The friars who accompanied him to his execution, however, prevented him from speaking by drenching him with holy water. In one disputed account, they smashed Grandier in the face with a heavy crucifix on the pretext of making him kiss it, thereby cruelly silencing him. The heinous prelates also fixed the garrotte so it could not be drawn tight enough for a successful strangulation. Father Lactance, one of Grandier's accusers, lit the bonfire and Jean De Laubardemont, a friend of the mother superior and an associate of Richelieu, gloated over the victim's agonies as he was consumed by fire. The man who supplied the stake and the firewood received 19 livres 16 sous for his pains. He signed a receipt for this fee on 24 August 1634.

Louis XIV had tried to ban burning but witchcraft came a little too close for comfort in the Affair of the Burning Room (*Chambre Ardente*) of 1673. Catherine Deshayes, who regularly supplied the aristocracy with arsenic and other poisons whenever they wished to quietly dispose of their former lovers, was the ringleader of a circle of devil worshippers. The Marquise De Montespan, the king's long-term mistress of twelve years, who feared she was losing influence over the king, attended three of these orgiastic 'love masses' and offered her naked body as the altar upon which the sacrilegious sacraments could be made. There was also evidence that she was procuring poison to murder the king's latest mistress.

On 22 February 1680, Madame Deshayes was taken to the stake 'tied and bound with iron. Cursing all the time, she was covered with straw, which five or six times she threw off her, but at last, the flames grew fiercer and she was lost to sight'. The Marquise De Montespan briefly returned to favour, only to be replaced by Madame De Maintenon, the middle-aged governess employed by the king to bring up her children.

Although witchcraft trials continued in France, actual burnings became rare: the usual cases involving priests who had seduced nuns in their charge and were consequently treated with leniency by the ecclesiastical authorities. Father Bertrand Guillaudot, however, who named twenty-nine accomplices, was burned in Dijon in 1742 for divination of treasure and necromancy. Five people were sentenced to death in Lyons in 1745 while the rest were banished or sent to the galleys. Father Louis Debaraz, who had officiated at sacrilegious masses, was the last man to be executed for witchcraft in France.

When it came to the burning of witches, Germany was home to a kind of pre-Holocaust, where at least 100,000 people were executed for witchcraft, usually by public burning. According to one 1590 chronicler in Wolfenbüttel, Brunswick, so many witches were burned that 'the place of execution looked like a small wood from the number of stakes'.

In August 1629, the chancellor of the Prince-Bishop of Würzburg wrote this chilling missive to an unnamed friend:

'As to this matter of witches, which Your Grace thought over some time ago, it has started up again and no words can adequately describe it. Ah, the woe and misery of it all. There are still four hundred in the city, high and low, of every rank and sex, even clergy, so strongly accused that they may be arrested at any minute. It is certain that many of the people of my gracious Prince-Bishop here, of all offices and faculties, must be executed: clerics, electoral councillors and doctors, city officials, court assessors, several of whom Your Grace knows. Law students have been arrested. My lord the Prince-Bishop has more than forty students who should soon become priests, of whom thirty or forty are said to be witches. A few days ago, a dean was arrested. Two others who were summoned have fled. A notary of our cathedral consistory, a very learned man, was arrested yesterday and put to the torture. In one word, a third of the city is surely implicated. The richest, most attractive, most prominent of the clergy are already executed. A week ago, a girl of nineteen was burned, of who it is said everywhere that she is the fairest in the whole city and was universally regarded as a girl of singular modesty and purity. In seven or eight days, she will be followed by others of the best and most attractive persons. Such people go in fresh mourning clothes undauntedly to their deaths, without a trace of fear of the flames. And thus many are burned for renouncing God and attending the witch dances, against whom nobody has ever else spoken a word. To conclude this horrible matter, there are three hundred children of three and four years, who are said to have intercourse with the devil. I have seen children of seven put to death and brave little students of ten, twelve, fourteen, and fifteen years of age. Of the nobles...– but I cannot write any more about this misery. There will yet be persons of higher rank, whom you may know and admire, and would scarcely believe it true of them. Let justice be done.'

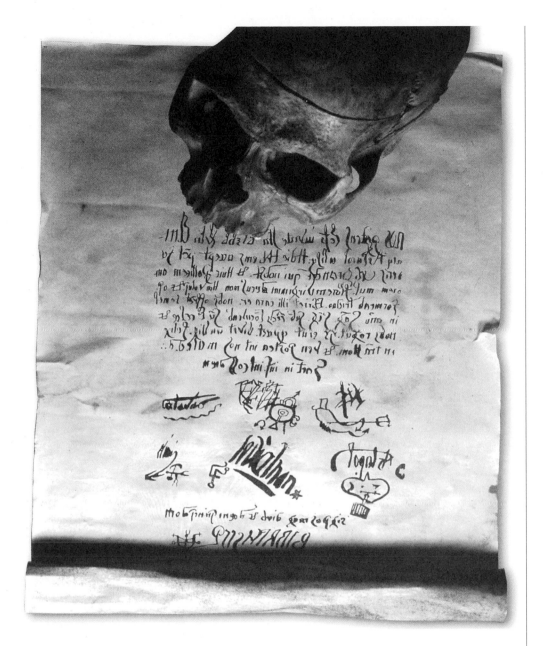

Left: The 'pact with the Devil' of Father Urbain Grandier, apparently signed by Beelzebub himself, and a number of other demons

Similar things were going on in Bonn, the official residence of the archbishop of Cologne. A priest named Duren from the village of Alfter, just outside of the city, wrote to Count Werner von Salm: 'That I haven't written for so long is because nothing unusual has happened, only that they have begun burning witches in Bonn'. He went on in his letter to explain the extent of the persecution:

'The victims of the funeral pyres are for the most part male. Half the city must be implicated for already professors, law students, pastors, canons, vicars, and monks have been arrested and burnt. His Prince Grace has seventy seminarians training to become priests, one of whom, eminent as a musician, was arrested yesterday; two others were sought but escaped. The chancellor and his wife and the private secretary's wife have already been apprehended and executed. On the Eve of Our

Lady's Day [7 September] there was executed here a girl of nineteen who had the reputation of being the loveliest and most virtuous in all the city, and who had been brought up by the Prince-Bishop himself. A canon of the cathedral named Rotensahe, I saw beheaded and burned. Children of three or four have devils for their paramours. Students and boys of noble birth of nine, ten, eleven, twelve, thirteen, and fourteen have been burnt here. To sum up, things are in a pitiful state, that one does not know with what people one may talk and associate.'

There were fewer witch trials in Cologne itself because the city council reserved the right to make arrests. In 1626, Catherine Henot, denounced by the nuns of St Clare for bewitching them, successfully defended her case before an ecclesiastical court when a counsel – a rarity in itself – argued that the evidence of demoniacs was inadmissible. Archbishop Ferdinand of Cologne then ordered a new trial before a secular court where Catherine Henot was found guilty and burned.

Right: A notable aspect of the heresy executions of the Middle Ages was the insistence of the Church on the repentance of the victim, even when already tied to the stake

In 1629, Christine Plum, a woman believed to be possessed, accused numerous others of witchcraft. When the priests hearing the trial plainly denounced her testimony as that of a mad person, they found themselves accused of the same charges. The archbishop encouraged such claims but the city council limited the number of arrests so persecution in Cologne never rivalled that in Bamberg, Würzburg, or Bonn.

Elsewhere in Germany, 1629 was a particularly bad year. At Miltenburg, in the archdiocese of Mainz, 178 people were executed in a township with a population of 3,000 whilst fifty-six individuals lost their lives in a nearby village. At Burgstädt – again with a population of less than 3,000 – seventy-seven citizens were burnt while another nineteen perished in the tiny village of Eichenbühel.

The situation was obviously out of control and the pope sent in two Italian cardinals, Albizzi and Giretti, to put an end to the madness. Upon arriving in the country in 1636, Albizzi wrote: 'A horrible spectacle met our eyes Outside the walls of many towns and villages, we saw numerous stakes to which poor wretched women were bound and burnt as witches'.

In the latter half of the eighteenth century, various German states began beheading witches, rather than burning them, unless it was clearly proven that the culprit had specifically entered into a pact with the devil. The last witch to be officially executed in Germany was Anna Maria Schwägel who died in Kempten, Bavaria in 1775. A servant girl and a Catholic, she was already in her mid-thirties and still single when she fell prey to a coachman who said he would marry her if she became a Lutheran. She travelled to Memmingen where she formally renounced Catholicism but, once the coachman had his way with her, he left her. Reverting back to her faith, she sought absolution from an Augustinian friar, only to discover that he, too, had converted to Protestantism after she had been pardoned. Believing this to be the work of the devil, she became crazed and wandered about the countryside, ending up in a mental asylum in Laneggen, near Kempton. The matron there, Anna Maria Kuhstaller, forced her to admit to having sex with the devil in the guise of the coachman before denouncing her before the magistrates. On 20 February 1775, the young woman was arrested and thrown into jail.

Her trial was held two weeks later. It seemed that no forms of torture had been used and, in her befuddled mental state, Anna Maria Schwägel freely admitted to having sex with the devil, fully awake and in her dreams, and to having made a pact with him. Even though no actual charges of *maleficia* were brought forward, the judges handed down a death sentence on 30 March but could not decide whether the victim ought to be burned, hanged, or beheaded. Honourius, Prince-Abbot of Kempten, examined her and simply advised, *'fiat justicia'* (let justice be carried out). Anna Maria Schwägel was beheaded on 11 April 1775.

C H A P T E R   7

The Reign of Terror

Before the French Revolution, a variety of methods were employed in putting a prisoner to death – regicides were quartered, thieves hanged, and highwaymen broken on the wheel. Only the privileged were despatched swiftly, if they were lucky, by beheading. The revolution extended this privilege to all social classes and ushered in an age when public execution was a swift and mechanized business. During the Reign of Terror that followed the French Revolution, it was performed efficiently and on an industrial scale by the guillotine.

The Ingenuity of Dr Guillotin

The man responsible for inventing this gruesome contraption was called Joseph-Ignace Guillotin. He was apparently born prematurely after his mother had gone into early labour in 1738 after hearing the screams of a man being broken on the wheel of the public scaffold at Saintes.

Guillotin was essentially a humane man who even considered taking holy orders before he became a physician. Elected to the National Assembly in 1789, he proposed a number of progressive measures concerning capital crime. Deputy Guillotin believed that criminal behaviour was a personal matter and that punishment and suffering should never be inflicted on the

Right: The guillotine. Despite its dreadful reputation, it was invented as a humane alternative to beheading with a sword, which frequently required more than one stroke

family of the condemned: they should be permitted to inherit the property of a felon, which ought never to be confiscated, and the body of an executed criminal should be returned to the family for burial, if they had requested it. Once burial had taken place, the parish register should withhold mentioning the sort of death the person had suffered. All these suggestions were well-received by the National Assembly.

Guillotin, however, had a further and more radical departure in mind. He was disgusted by exhibitions of bodies in gibbets and believed felons should go to their death with the least possible misery involved. Beheading fitted the bill. In keeping with the new democratic and egalitarian sentiments of the French Revolution, all deaths should be the same: decapitation, previously reserved for the privileged class, should be extended to all. Yet Guillotin was well aware that, even with a skilled executioner, beheading was a hit-and-miss affair and he managed to get a motion passed by the National Assembly requiring death sentences to be carried out 'by means of a machine'.

Various designers were considered, including those of the Scottish Maiden and the Halifax Gibbet. The most advanced machine at the time was the Italian *Mannaïa* where an axe descended between two perpendicular slipboards. This device had been first tried out in France in 1631 during Marshal De Montmorency's execution in Toulouse.

For expert advice, Guillotin naturally turned to the official executioner

Below: The Halifax Gibbet, the precursor to the French guillotine, in action.

himself, Charles-Henri Sanson. The problem with beheadings, Sanson informed him, was that the felon often lacked the 'firmness which was absolutely necessary for such executions', which was understandable given the circumstances. If the victim fainted while kneeling, he or she fell sideways, blunting the effect of the first swing of the sword. Sanson insisted that the solution was to keep the victim's body horizontal.

One evening, Sanson discussed the problem with his friend Schmidt, a German instrument maker, who proceeded to sketch the design of what would later become the world-famous guillotine. Guillotin was enthusiastic. At a sitting of the National Assembly on 30 April 1791, he told his fellow deputies that the felon would feel only 'a slight freshness on the back of the neck', adding that, 'with this machine, I chop your head off in a twinkling, and you do not suffer'. The house broke into laughter.

Even so, the assembly appointed the king's physician, Dr Antoine Louis, to evaluate the design. A keen locksmith, the king, too, had a passion for

Right: The Frenchman Dr Guillotin, who combined various forms of 'beheading machines' to perfect the guillotine

machinery and wanted to examine the design himself. He was impressed but expressed doubts about the shape of the blade which, in the original design, was a crescent. Sanson was consulted and he agreed that an oblique edge would be better. Both versions would be put to the test.

On 20 March 1792, Dr Louis was instructed to go ahead and commission the first prototype of this decapitation machine from a carpenter called Guidon for 5,500 francs. When it was finished, Sanson and two of his brothers tried it out on three corpses in the courtyard of the prison at Bicêtre. The first two strikes with an oblique edge were successful but the third with a crescent-shaped edge was not. Hence the version with the oblique knife stuck.

On 25 April 1792, the new machine was tried out in public for the first time at the Place de Grève. The victim was a highwayman named Pelletin, who fell into a dead faint, so it would have been impossible to behead him by sword in the conventional way. With the victim prone, the descending blade did its work and the experiment proved a great success.

At this time, the device was called a *louison* or *louisette* after Dr Louis and only later became known as *la guillotine*. For the first seven months, it was used to despatch common thieves and forgers but the political situation in France was rapidly becoming volatile. On 20 August 1792, the Tuileries Palace was invaded and the king himself was arrested.

Soon after, a forger named Cobot was to be executed. Sanson set up the guillotine in the Place de Grève but the radical Jacobin insisted that it be moved to the Place du Carousel, where it would be closer to the Tuileries. By the time the guillotine reached the new location, Cobot was in a frenzy and Sanson asked for the execution to be delayed until he had calmed down. A beardless youth with a red cap threatened Sanson: if he did not quickly carry on with the execution, he would get a taste of the guillotine himself.

Sanson replied that he could not execute the man without the help of his assistants. Surveying the mob, the young revolutionary suggested, 'you can find as much help as you require here. The blood of aristocrats cements the happiness of the nation, and there is not one man in the crowd who is not ready to lend you a hand'. There was a general cry of assent.

The culprit refused to mount the scaffold so Sanson had to carry him bodily up the steps. As soon as Cobot saw the guillotine, he begged for mercy. The crowd fell silent. Sanson again asked for a delay but the young revolutionary would not back down. After a brief struggle, the two men managed to strap the criminal to the base plank. Sanson told his new assistant that he could provide no better proof of his patriotism than to perform the execution himself. The young man pulled the rope, releasing the blade; the knife descended and the head rolled into the basket. Sanson asked his newfound collaborator to pick up the head and show it to the crowd. When he reached the edge of the scaffold and held the head aloft, the youth staggered and fell backwards. Thinking he had fainted, Sanson went to help him but the young man was dead from an apoplectic fit which killed him instantly. The paroxysm had been caused by the violent emotions stirred in him during the execution.

As Sanson had been the king's executioner under the old regime, he was suspected of being a royalist and the authorities kept a close eye on him. The all-powerful prosecutor, Antoine Quentin Fouquier-Tinville, asked him why he did not pull the rope that released the knife that actually executed the victim – after all, he had wielded the sword in the days before the guillotine. Sanson replied that pulling the rope was purely a mechanical function. Preparing the victim and overseeing the whole operation was more important if accidents were to be avoided. Fouquier-Tinville seemed satisfied with this answer, although he warned that if Sanson neglected his duties, he would be sent to the guillotine. After a subsequent shift in politics, it was Fouquier-Tinville who found himself there.

The Execution of Louis XVI

On 20 January 1793, Sanson received the order to erect a guillotine in the Place de la Révolution (modern-day Place de la Concorde) for the execution of Louis XVI the following day. He also received an unsigned letter declaring that the king would be rescued and asking him to delay the execution for as long as possible in order to allow men loyal to the king to break through the crowds. A third anonymous letter threatened him if he tried to thwart any rescue attempt. Charles-Henri was assisted in the momentous task of executing Louis XVI by his two brothers, Charlemagne, the executioner of Provins, and Louis Martin, the executioner of Tours. He left this account:

'I started out at seven o'clock in the morning, after embracing my poor wife who I did not expect to see again. I rode in a carriage with my brothers, Charlemagne and Louis Martin. The crowd in the streets was so large that it was close upon nine o'clock before we reached the Place de la Révolution. Gors and Barré, my assistants, had erected the guillotine, and I was so persuaded that it would not be used that I hardly looked at it. My brothers were well armed, and so was I; under our coats we had, besides our swords, daggers, four pistols, and a flask of powder, and our pockets were full of bullets. We felt sure that some attempt would be made to rescue the king, and we intended, if we could, to assist in saving his life.

'When we reached the Place, I looked about for my son, and I discovered him at a short distance with his battalion. He nodded and seemed to encourage me. I listened intently for some indication as to what was about to occur. I rejoiced at the thought that the king had perhaps been rescued on the way, and that he was already beyond the reach of danger. However, as my eyes were bent in the direction of the Madeleine, I suddenly espied a body of cavalry which was coming up at a trot and,

immediately after it, a carriage drawn by two horses and surrounded by a double row of horsemen. No doubt could now exist; the victim was at hand. My sight became dim and I looked at my son; he also was deadly pale.

'The carriage stopped at the foot of the scaffold. The king was sitting on the back seat on the right; next to him was his confessor and on the front seat two gendarmes. The latter came down first; then the priest stepped out, and he was directly followed by the king who appeared even more collected and calm than when I saw him at Versailles and the Tuileries.*

'As he approached the steps of the scaffold, I cast a glance around. The people were silent, the drums were sounding, and there was not the slightest sign of a rescue being at hand. Charlemagne was as troubled as I was; as to my brother Martin, he was younger and had more firmness. He advanced respectfully, took off his hat, and told the king that he must take his coat off. "There is no need," he answered.*

Below: King Louis XVI of France meets his end on the guillotine. His reputation as a bloodthirsty tyrant is largely down to propaganda, however

"Despatch me as I am now." My brother insisted, and added that it was indispensably necessary to bind his hands. The last observation moved him greatly. He reddened and exclaimed, "What! Would you dare to touch me? Here is my coat, but do not lay a finger on me!" After saying that, he took off his coat. Charlemagne came to Martin's assistance and, scarcely knowing how to address the illustrious victim, he said, in a cold tone which could hardly conceal his profound emotion, "It is absolutely necessary. The execution cannot proceed otherwise."

'In my turn I interfered, and bending close to the ear of the priest, I whispered, "Monsieur l'Abbé, ask the king to submit. While I tie his hands we can gain time and perhaps some assistance may be forthcoming". The abbé looked sadly and eagerly in my face, and then addressing the king: "Sire," he said, "submit to the last sacrifice, which shall make you look more like our Saviour."

'The king held out his hands while his confessor was presenting the crucifix to his lips. Two assistants tied the hands which had wielded the sceptre. He then ascended the steps of the scaffold, supported by the worthy priest. "Are the drums going to sound forever?" he said to Charlemagne. On reaching the platform, he advanced to the side where the crowd was the thickest and made such an imperative sign that the drummers stopped for a moment. "Frenchmen!" he exclaimed, in a strong voice, "you see your king ready to die for you. May my blood cement your happiness! I die innocent of what I am charged with!" He was about to continue when Antoine Joseph Santerre, who was in command of the proceedings, ordered the drummers to beat and nothing more could be heard. In a moment, he was bound to the plank, and a few seconds afterwards when, at the touch of my hand the blade was sliding down, he could still hear the voice of the priest pronouncing the words: "Son of Saint-Louis, ascend to Heaven!"

'Thus died the unfortunate prince who might have been saved by a thousand well-armed men; and really I am at a loss to understand the notice which I received the day before the execution that some attempt at rescue would be made. The slightest signal would have been sufficient to cause a diversion in his favour; for if when Gros, my assistant, showed the king's head to the multitude some cries of triumph were uttered [but] the greater part of the crowd turned away with profound horror.'

Abbé Firmont, the royal confessor, also left this account of his monarch's last moments:

'At first, an awful silence prevailed; at length, some cries of "Vive La République!" [Long Live the Republic] were heard. By degrees the voices multiplied, and in less than ten minutes, this cry, a thousand times repeated, became the universal shout of the multitude and every hat was in the air'.

Soon the gloating mob was soaking handkerchiefs in the king's blood. Charles-Henri Sanson was so troubled by what he saw that he sought out a priest to conduct an expiatory secret mass in a derelict house.

Left: Marie Antoinette on her way to the guillotine. As an Austrian and an aristocrat, she was doubly unpopular with the French crowd

Marie-Antoinette

The following year, Sanson was called upon to execute Queen Marie Antoinette. As an Austrian, she was doubly unpopular and was taunted by crowds all the way to the guillotine. Sanson supported her as she made her way up onto the scaffold. On the plank she was heard saying 'farewell my children, I am going to join your father' in a loud voice.

The Republican journalist Jacques Rene Hébert, chief spokesman for the extremely radical *sansculottes* (so-called because they wore trousers or pantaloons instead of the aristocratic knee breeches), rejoiced at the queen's execution. 'All of you who have been oppressed by our former tyrants,' he wrote, 'you who mourn a father, son, or a husband who has died for the republic, take comfort, for you are avenged. I saw the head to the female Austrian fall into the sack. I wish to God I could describe the satisfaction of the *sansculottes* when the arch-tigress drove across Paris in the carriage with thirty-six doors.' [The cart that brought the condemned to the scaffold had thirty-six slats – and gaps between them – along the sides.]

'She was not pulled by her beautiful white horses with their fine feathers and their grand harnesses but by a couple of nags harnessed to Master Sanson's barouche,

and they were apparently so glad to contribute to the deliverance of the republic that they seemed anxious to gallop to reach the fatal spot more quickly. The jade, however, remained bold and insolent to the end. But her legs failed her as she got upon the seesaw to play hot-cockles [a comical reference to the choking sound made by victims], in the fear, no doubt, of finding a more terrible punishment before her, after death, than the one she was about to endure. Her accursed head was at last separated from her crane-like neck and the air was filled with cries of "Vive La République!" '

Five months later, Hébert himself went to the guillotine whilst Charles-Henri Sanson survived it all. He retired on 30 October 1795 and his son Henri took over as the executioner of Paris, though he was not formally confirmed in the post until Charles-Henri died in 1806. Between them, during the revolutionary period, they beheaded nearly 3,000 people.

The Terror Spreads

The executions were not confined to Paris. On 5 September 1793, the revolutionary government issued a decree making 'terror' the order of the day. The enemies of the revolution – nobles, churchmen, and those suspected of hoarding food and private property – were to be eliminated. On 17 September, the Committee of Public Safety under Maximilien Robespierre passed the Law of Suspects which allowed them to arrest and execute anyone suspected of harbouring anti-revolutionary views. The revolutionary army was sent from Paris out into the countryside with a mobile guillotine, conscription was introduced, and soon the army was half-a-million strong. 'Now, a river of blood will divide France from its enemies,' said Robespierre.

The revolution was a product of the so-called Age of Reason and organized religion was seen as the enemy. The committee sent agents out across the country to de-Christianize the population. Churches and cemeteries were vandalized. The Bishop of Paris was forced to resign whilst Notre Dame was deconsecrated and renamed the Temple of Reason. The old calendar was scrapped on 5 October 1793 in favour of new 'rational' systems, free from Christian associations. There were to be twelve months, each made up of three ten-day weeks, beginning from 22 September 1792 (the date of the formal establishment of the republic) which was to be 1 Vendémiaire, year I.

Not everyone was in favour of the revolution's excesses. Lyon rebelled but on 9 October, after a bloody bombardment, the revolutionaries retook the city and renamed it *Ville Affranchie* (Liberated Town). The houses of the rich were demolished and twenty to thirty rebels were executed. Suspicious that the local Lyonnais Revolutionaries were being too lenient on their fellow townspeople, they sent in a Jacobin zealot named Mathieu Parein. He

Left: Georges Danton, revolutionary hero, falls foul of Robespierre after pleading for a halt to the endless executions of the Terror

ordered those with an income of 30,000 livres or more to hand over their money and for all vestiges of religion to be obliterated. Houses were searched and the mass executions began.

The guillotine became overworked. On 11 Nivôse, year II (according to the new revolutionary calendar), thirty-two heads were severed in twenty-five minutes. A week later, twelve heads were severed in just five minutes. This was a messy method for disposing of one's political enemies and the residents of rue Lafont, where the guillotine was set up, kept complaining about the blood overflowing from the drainage ditch that ran underneath the scaffold.

Mass shootings also took place. As many as sixty prisoners were tied up in a line with ropes and shot at with cannon. Those who were not killed outright were finished off with bayonets, sabres, and rifles. The chief butcher, an actor named Dorfeuille, wrote to Paris boasting that he had killed 113 Lyonnais in a single day. Three days later, he butchered 209 people and he promised that another four or five hundred would 'expiate their crimes with fire and shot'. This was grossly underestimated. By the time the killing had stopped, the death toll was 1,905 and the victims were not restricted to the rich, the aristocratic, and the clergy. The unemployed were also liquidated, along with

Above: Crowds at the guillotine. As with public executions at Tyburn, beheadings in France were festive affairs

anyone the Revolutionary Tribunal decided was a *'fanatique'*.

Marseilles – now the *Ville Sans Nom* (Town Without A Name) – was similarly purged. After an insurrection in the Vendée, western France, the local agent wrote to the Committee of Public Safety in Paris describing their reprisals. 'There is no more Vendée, citizens,' he announced. 'It has just perished under our free sword along with its women and children. I have just buried it in the marshes and mud of Savenay. Following the orders you gave me, I have crushed children under the feet of horses and massacred women who at least will give birth to no more brigands. I have no prisoners with which to reproach myself.' The name Vendée was changed to *Vengé* (Avenged).

Two hundred prisoners were executed in Angers in December alone and 2,000 more at Saint-Florent. At Pont-de-Cé and Avrillé, 3–4,000 victims were shot in one long, relentless slaughter. At Nantes, the guillotine was so overworked that a new method of public execution, known as 'vertical deportation', was devised. A flat-bottomed barrage would be holed below the waterline, then a plank nailed over the hole to keep the boat temporarily afloat. Prisoners were put on the barge with their hands and feet tied together. The barge would be taken out into the middle of the Loire River, where the executioner would pull out the plank and jump to safety on board a boat that was floating alongside the other vessel. The barge would sink, taking the prisoners down with it. Anyone attempting to escape drowning would be hacked to death with sabres.

This form of execution was at first reserved for clerics and known as a 'republican baptism'. Later the term 'national bath' was more widely used. Prisoners were often stripped of their clothes and young men and women were sometimes tied together naked and given a 'republican marriage'.

The revolutionary army spread out across the country looking for sedition. They would slaughter men, women, and children they suspected of harbouring anti-Jacobin sympathies. Crops were also burned, farm animals slaughtered, barns and cottages demolished, and woods torched. Any town or village that had entertained anti-Jacobin troops would be razed to the ground. Terrorists planned to put arsenic in wells and enquires were made of a well-known chemist about the possibilities of developing poison gas.

Twelve infernal columns were sent to 'pacify' the countryside by killing everyone in their path. Women were raped, children killed, both were mutilated. Entire families were found swimming in their own blood. One impeccable republican lost three of his sons plus his son-in-law on the first visit of the Jacobins. They returned to massacre his remaining son, his wife, and their fifteen-year-old daughter. To save on ammunition, General Cordeiller ordered his men to use the sabre instead of the gun.

At Gonnord, General Crouzat forced 200 elderly people to kneel in front of the pit they had just dug with the help of mothers and children. Victims were shot so they fell into the new grave. Some tried to make a break for it but were struck down by the hammer of a local mason. Thirty children and two women were buried alive when earth was finally shovelled into the pit.

In the Loire Valley, around a quarter of a million people were killed – one-third of the region's population! This figure does not include those who lost their lives in the revolution or during the subsequent wars fighting on the side of the republicans.

Thanks to the Law of Suspects, Parisian prisons were full to overflowing. The rich were made to pay for their board and lodging. The guillotine was being overworked, too. A prostitute was executed for expressing royalist sentiments – she had complained that trade had fallen off since the revolution. When one prisoner stabbed himself to death in front of the Revolutionary Tribunal, the court ordered that his corpse be guillotined anyway. Revolutionary justice was not to be cheated.

The revolution then began to consume its own. Anyone who opposed Robespierre was sentenced to 'look through the republican window' – that is, put his head through the frame of the guillotine. When the great revolutionary hero Georges Danton tried to call a halt to the terror, he, too, was arrested and sent to be 'shaved by the national razor'. Entire families were guillotined, the older members being forced to watch the younger ones being executed while awaiting their turn.

Robespierre saw himself as a righteous, virtuous missionary and believed that he was using the guillotine as an instrument of the nation's moral improvement. The de-Christianizers, whom Robespierre viewed as immoral, paid for his views with their lives. He instituted the Festival of the Supreme Being in which he took on a leading role. This was not a return to believing in God, he explained. Nature was the 'Supreme Being' but many questioned whether Robespierre really thought that the supreme being was himself.

The new crimes of 'slandering patriotism', 'seeking to inspire discouragement', 'spreading false news', 'depraving morals', 'corrupting the public conscience', and 'impairing the purity and energy of the Revolutionary government' were introduced. To speed up the course of justice, the accused were allowed no defence counsel and no witnesses would be called to the stand. The jury was made up of law-abiding citizens who were more than capable of coming to a fair and unbiased judgement without being distracted by such trifles. There were only two outcomes – acquittal or death – which usually meant death. Robespierre himself coined the slogan: 'Clemency is parricide'. Executions jumped from five a day in the new revolutionary month of Germinal to twenty-six a day in Messidor, year II.

Things had been going well for the French army and any danger from abroad had eased off for the time being. Some republicans began to question the need for such Draconian measures. Anyone who opposed this new revolutionary justice must certainly have something to hide, Robespierre argued, and promptly investigated these people. He was so busy organizing the persecution that he did not realize that leading revolutionaries were mocking his cult of the Supreme Being behind his back.

On 26 July 1794 (8 Thermidor, year II), Robespierre made a speech calling for 'more virtue' and his supporters called for his enemies to be sent *'à la guillotine'* (to the guillotine). The next day, critics pointed out that Robespierre had departed from protocol – instead of speaking for the collective leadership, he made a speech in his own name. He was lost for words at this accusation. In the silence, a voice piped up: 'See, the blood of Danton chokes him'.

Robespierre's opponents swiftly moved against him. He and his supporters were arrested and could hardly ask for clemency. After a failed suicide attempt which left him with a shattered jaw, Robespierre and seventeen of his followers were guillotined. A fastidious little man, he went to the scaffold covered in dry blood. The bandage that was holding up his jaw was yanked off to avoid obstructing the blade. He yelped in pain, only to be silenced by the guillotine. The executioner was Charles-Henri Sanson.

The death figures from this dark period of history are truly staggering:

leas
die

CHAPTER 8

Exotic Executions

In 1866, two British army officers, R. Mounteney Jephson and Edward Pennell Elmhirst, were invited by the governor of Kanagawa jail to witness the gruesome business of a Japanese execution. It began with a ceremonial procession. 'First of all came two men bearing placards raised on poles,' read their account, 'the one proclaiming the nature of the crime for which the offender was going to suffer and the punishment he was condemned to undergo; the other inscribed with his name and native place.' According to the placard, the condemned man was being executed for having broken into a house.

'Immediately following rode the doomed man, tied to his horse, with his arms tightly pinioned behind him, and a rope fastened to his waist, held by a man who walked alongside. Never had it been our luck before, and we trust it may never be again, to behold a creature in God's image reduced to such a state. With a skin blanched, parched, and shrivelled; features worn and distorted; eyeballs glazed and sunk; his cheekbones appearing to be forcing themselves out, and his withered arms hanging nerveless at his side, the wretched being strove hard to bear himself bravely, and to behave to the last as became one of his race. As he passed, his eye lit on our party, and he called out, with a scornful laugh, for "the foreigners to come and see how a Nippon could die". A year in a Japanese prison – a year of torture and starvation – had brought what was said to have been once a fine, powerful man to the repulsive and wasted form now before us; yet his heart had not died out, nor his pluck deserted him, and he could still hurl defiance at his hated persecutors.'

The British officers compared the fortitude of the Japanese to that of the Spartans and Roman foot soldiers.

'Next in order in the procession came two spearmen; then some men on foot; and lastly, two officers on horseback with their retainers.'

The officers were ushered into the prison and its central courtyard which was surrounded by cages that left the prisoners inside them exposed to the elements. 'Fearful tales are told of the tortures employed to extort confession or punish crimes. The coloured drawings of the Japanese (and we have been informed by various good authorities that they are no exaggeration) reveal scenes and phases of human suffering almost too dreadful to dwell upon. The fiendish ingenuity of the Roman Inquisition is outdone by the diabolical contrivances of the acknowledged jurisdiction of Japan.

'Thieving, more particularly when accompanied by violence, stands almost highest in the list of crimes; and for this, in its worst forms, are reserved some of the most cruel tortures. Death – the shape to be determined by the amount stolen and the way the offence is perpetrated – is the punishment for robbery of anything over the value of forty ichiboos [about sixty shillings – £3 – or £185 in today's money]. Confession, wrung out in sweating agony – too often, 'tis to be feared, from an innocent man – by means of the bastinado, *by the application of crushing weights piled gradually heavier and still heavier on the yielding chest; by severing member after member, and limb after limb, from the quivering trunk, by —— we forebear to sicken you by enumerating other tortures, if possible, more terrible and cruel still – may be followed by beheading, by crucifixion, by impalement on blunt spears, by tearing asunder by means of wild cattle, rendered mad by flaming torches, or by some other of the many awful forms of death at disposal.*

'While we had been making our tour of inspection, the doomed culprit had been

Above: Double execution in Yokohama, Japan. Each man was beheaded with a single stroke of the sword

unlashed, and dismounted from his horse at the gate; but, when set on his feet, he was unable, from weakness and the constraint and painful position in which he had been kept so long, to stand; and they were obliged to carry him into the precincts of the prison. Here an ample breakfast had been provided, and any kind of refreshment he chose to ask for was allowed him. This would appear to be a heartless mockery, as if it were intended to ridicule the poor wretch in his last moments; but, on the contrary, he applied himself vigorously to the meal, the completion of which was to be the signal for his own leap into eternity.'

As the man had been malnourished for at least a year, he ate heartily 'and the sufferings he had gone through had rendered his mind callous to the last punishment, or made death appear but a happy escape'. It was then that he caught sight of the onlookers. He saluted them politely enough but turned to his guards and cursed the *bocca tojins* (foreign fools).

'When a full half hour had elapsed, it was intimated to him that his presence was now expected; and accordingly with the assistance of an attendant on each side, he walked slowly into the execution ground, and was placed, kneeling and sitting on his heels (in the universal Japanese posture), behind a small hole dug out for the

reception of his head. Some ten yards in front of him, and separated by a rope running across the square, sat the presiding yakonin *and the prison authorities, calmly fanning themselves; and beyond these, again, were the six or eight foreigners who had been admitted.*

'*The prisoner's arms were pinioned behind his back but, before the cloth was tied over his eyes, he requested that a minute's grace be allowed him. This being granted, he raised a weak, quavering voice to its highest pitch, and screamed out, "My Friends!" Immediately an unearthly chorus of wails answered the poor wretch from his friends outside the walls, none of whom could be seen from the interior. The effect of this was positively startling to the nerves of us strangers: Mr L— [their interpreter] alone was at all prepared and explained to us the meaning of what passed. "Friends!" again shouted the unfortunate man – and after each sentence the same thrilling response was sent back to him – "I am about to die but think not that I care!" a horrible attempt at a laugh following the last words. "Do not mind me! It is quite indifferent to me! Rather look out for yourselves! Sayonara (goodbye)!" and, with a deeper more prolonged wail, the crowd outside answered, "Sayonara!"*

'*He then signalled to his guards that he was ready and submitted quickly to the operation of the blindfolding. The executioner, who had hitherto been standing by his side – with the greatest* sang froid *pouring water on the keen blade of his long two-handed sword – now stepped up, and carefully adjusting his head a little on one side, and in such a position as to hand exactly over the hole prepared to receive it, signed to the officer that all was prepared; but before the latter would give the signal – and while the wretched being before us was momentarily expecting the death stroke – he inquired of Mr L — with every mark of politeness, if the English officers were ready. Of course he quickly answered, "Yes," and the word was given – when, without raising his weapon more than a foot above the neck of the condemned, the executioner brought down his heavy blade with a plainly audible thud and the head dropped instantly into the place prepared for it.*

'*We had always fancied ourselves possessed of very fair nerves but we must confess to a most sickening feeling as the dull splash of the sword meeting its victim – turning at that instant living flesh into senseless clay – struck on our ears, and the cleaving of the neck showed for a moment a ghastly red circle, with the blood leaping out in streams from the headless trunk. As we turned to look at the others of our little group, we could see by the whitened faces of the strong men around that they, too, were not altogether unaffected by the scene they had just witnessed.*'

As soon as the head fell, it was picked up, washed, and placed in a bag. At the same time that this was happening, two men would squeeze the decapitated body while it was still warm to extract the remaining blood. The body was then rolled up, tied up in a bundle, and taken away. The procession formed again, this time with the executioner riding the horse that had previously carried the condemned man, and conveyed the head to a location about one mile away where a kind of gallows had been erected to display the severed head for six days as a warning to others.

Jephson and Elmhirt admitted to being surprised by their reactions to the witnessed execution. A year or so before, they had seen the beheading of three Chinese in Canton,

'where it is of such daily occurrence, and is thought so little of, that in one corner of the execution ground some scores of heads – without any exaggeration – may always be seen piled in all stages of preservation or corruption. But there is was done in such a business-like, informal way, and the Chinamen seemed to be so little affected by their approaching fate – actually laughing and talking till their moment when, as they knelt down, their tails were pulled forward and the short, heavy sword took their heads off one by one – that we looked upon it in quite a different light from the scene we have just described, nor experienced any of the disagreeable sensations as on that occasion'.

The Death of a Thousand Cuts

In 1865, other members of their regiment had witnessed the terrible fate of the rebel chief Mowung in Canton after he had been handed over by the acting governor of Hong Kong. The mandarins condemned him as a traitor and sentenced him to the death of twenty-one cuts 'by which, before the last stroke lets out together his quivering bowels and his life, each of the previous twenty severs a fresh portion of flesh and muscle from the wretched sufferer. With superhuman command of self, the unhappy Mowung bore silently the slow, deliberate slicing off – first of his cheeks, then of his breasts, the muscles of upper and lower arms, the calves of his legs…care being taken throughout to avoid touching any immediately vital part. Once only he murmured an entreaty that he might be killed outright – a request of course unheeded by men who took a savage pleasure in skilfully torturing their victim'.

The Chinese interpreter to HM Consulate Thomas Taylor Meadows also witnessed the 'death of a thousand cuts' when thirty-four rebels or bandits were to be executed on 30 July 1851: 'A hole in the ground near to which a rough cross leant against the wall showed me that one man at least was going to suffer the highest legal punishment – cutting up live, called *ling-chy*, a disgraceful and lingering death,' he wrote.

'As soon as the thirty-three were decapitated, the same executioner proceeded, with a single-edged dagger or knife, to cut up the man on the cross, whose sole clothing consisted of wide trousers, rolled down to his hips and up to his buttocks. He was a strongly made man, about middle size, and apparently about forty years old. The authorities had captured him by seizing his parents and wife when he surrendered, as well as to save them from torture as to secure for them the seven thousand dollars

for his apprehension. As the man was at a distance of twenty-five yards with his side towards us, though he observed the two cuts across his forehead, the cutting off of his left breast and slicing of the flesh from the front of his thighs, we could not see all the horrible operation. From the first stroke of the knife till the moment he was cut down from the cross and decapitated, about four or five minutes elapsed. We should not have been prohibited from going close up, but as may be easily imagined, even a powerful curiosity was insufficient inducement to jump over a number of dead bodies and literally wade through pools of blood to place ourselves in the hearing of the groans indicated by the heaving chest and quivering limbs of the poor man. Where we stood, we heard not a single cry...'

There were certainly not a thousand cuts. The exact number depended on the severity of the crime. There were as few as eight before clemency was called for or there could be as many as 120. But twenty-five seems to have been the average.

Traditionally, the victim was tied to a cross that was next to a table with a basket of razor-sharp knives covered by a cloth. Each knife was marked with the Chinese character for a particular part of the body. The executioner reached into the basket and underneath the cloth to pull out a knife. After reading the name, he began working on that body part. The victim got lucky and mercifully died only when the executioner pulled out the knife with the character for 'heart' inscribed on it. However, it seems this method was later modified and only one knife used when amputating the parts of the body in a strict order.

In 1895, Sir Henry Norman witnessed this method being carried out. Once the victim was secured to the cross, the executioner 'grasping handfuls from the fleshy parts of the body, such the thighs and the breasts' sliced them off. The 'joints and excrescences of the body' were cut away, one by one, followed by the amputation of the nose, fingers, and toes. He started to work on the wrists and ankles, amputating the hands and feet, 'then the limbs are cut off piecemeal at the wrists and the ankles, the elbows and knees, the shoulders and hip. Finally the victim is stabbed in the heart and his head cut off'. Death by the 'slicing process' was still being used in public executions during the Communist rebellion of 1929.

Human Sacrifice

In pre-Columbian Mexico, gruesome deaths were not solely reserved for criminals but were offered as sacrifices to placate the gods and keep the universe in balance. As huge numbers of public deaths were needed, the Aztec warriors went to war and captured as many victims as possible: these battles were largely ceremonial affairs with elaborate costumes and the soldiers carried only one weapon, a small sword made of obsidian or volcanic glass. The object was to capture as many of the enemy as possible for use in human sacrifice. In order to do this, only the leader was captured or killed so the surviving army would be forced to capitulate.

Captives would be taken up to the highest levels of the great Aztec temple pyramids and laid on the sacrificial altars in a supine position. Minor priests would restrain the victims while the high priest slit open the chests and pulled out the still-beating hearts. Such sacrifices were thought necessary to sustain the sun's transit through the sky and precious sacrificial blood was collected into ceremonial bowls. Heads were piled on specially designed skull racks and the high priest and other dignitaries would dress themselves in the flayed skins of their victims.

When the Spanish turned up in the Aztec capital of Tenochtitlán (modern-day Mexico City) in 1519, they witnessed the festival of the Aztec

Below: Aztec ritual sacrifice of prisoners of war. The still-beating heart was torn out of the unfortunate victim's chest, as a sacrifice to the sun god

Right: St Stephen, the first Christian martyr, is stoned to death, c. AD 33. Regrettably, this barbaric method of execution is still practised in certain parts of the world

war god Huitzilopochtli which, like all Aztec festivals, involved human sacrifice on an epic scale. Horrified by these bloodthirsty practices, the Spaniards turned on the Aztecs and slaughtered as many as 10,000 priests and worshippers. This aggression precipitated a war with the Spanish which the Aztecs inevitably lost as they had no immunity to smallpox, a disease unknown to the natives.

There were other horrible and humiliating ways to die. Stoning, for example, was the Biblical punishment for sodomy and fornication: a particularly public form of execution, it required the active participation of onlookers. During the religious fervour of the seventeenth century this form of torture experienced a revival. Ecclesiastical records detail the sorry fate of Mistress Clementine, whose husband found her in bed with another man. She was dragged from her room to the justices and from there on to the market square where a crowd had gathered. After being stripped naked, she was tied to a post. Her husband was asked to cast the first stone but he declined. The rest of the crowd started stoning her: they hurled rocks and bricks for half an hour. Although their aim was good, they failed to land a fatal blow until a jagged piece of rock hit her full in the face. Her eyes suddenly glazed over, her head dropped, and she was proclaimed dead. Her body was cut from head to foot and her breasts reduced to a pulp. An executioner holding a cudgel stood by in case the stones failed to do the job.

The Ibo people of Nigeria devised an ingenious punishment for adultery. The guilty couple were stripped naked, tied together, and forced to copulate in front of the whole village, to the sound of derisive hoots, whistles, and the sound of drums. Long wooden stakes were then driven through them and the unhappy pair were thrown to the crocodiles to be eaten.

Another African tribe employed the most brutal form of punishment imaginable for adultery. The naked couple were starved and bound to two posts about four feet apart, with only salt water to drink. On the first day, the village would look on as the executioner cut off a piece of the woman and forced her lover to eat it. The executioner's assistant would staunch the blood from her wound. On the second day, a portion of the man's flesh was removed and fed to the woman. The executioner would take great pride in avoiding major organs and keeping the victims alive. The procedure would continue until one of them died. Most horrifyingly of all, the person who had 'survived' was forced to continue eating human flesh until they, too, expired.

The practice of flaying people alive dates back to the time of the Assyrians. The victim was tied to a stake and the skin removed in strips until the flesh underneath lay fully exposed. In 1366, the chamberlain of the Count de Rouci was killed in this fashion while Paolo Garnier was castrated before the flaying actually began. In 1655, during the persecution of the Waldenses, brothers David and Jacopo Perrin had the skin on their arms and legs stripped off.

CHAPTER 9

Military Methods

Traditionally, the military have executed soldiers by firing squad. The practice was regarded as an honourable death for any fighting man, akin to facing the enemy's bullets. Being shot in the back of the head was a more reliable method and, in many ways, a better way to go. Regardless of the fact that it brought an instant and painless death because the medulla (the seat of consciousness) was irreparably damaged, it was, however, less highly regarded.

The Firing Squad

A firing squad customarily comprised three to six shooters for every prisoner. These men stood or knelt opposite the victim. Tied to a post or propped up against a wall, human targets were usually given the choice of being blindfolded or looking bravely into the face of death. It was common practice to load up one of the guns at random with a blank cartridge. No one in the firing squad knew where in the magazine the blank was lodged so soldiers could pretend they were not firing a fatal shot and absolve themselves of a little guilt.

The impact of a bullet tearing into the body cavity, rupturing skin and fracturing bones would have caused the victim's body to heat up, boiling off water and fat, and leaving a hole ten times the size of the original point of entry. Members of the firing squad were trained to aim at the person's chest – a larger target area than the head. The victim would experience a sensation that was rather like being punched or stung. The acute pain came only later if he or she was still alive. If the bullet hit the heart, the person died quickly through shock and internal haemorrhage; if the lungs were targeted, the victim asphyxiated; if the firing squad missed any of the major organs, an officer or NCO was on standby to administer the *coup de grace* – a pistol shot to the head. Even that may not have proven fatal.

In 1915, a Mexican student called Wenceslao Moguel was captured after a group of rebels tried to take over a province in the Yucatán peninsula. He was nicknamed *'El Fusilado'* after a firing squad failed to despatch him – even though he had been hit eight times and shot in the head once by the officer in charge. 'After many hours of fighting, the government forces took us prisoner,' he told a journalist. 'We were all sentenced to death summarily and faced the firing squad in pairs.'

When his turn came, Moguel tried to think of something to give him courage. His throat went dry as he gazed at the firing squad who appeared to be staring back at him with equal intensity. In the final moments, the image of St James came into his mind and he prayed for a miracle. 'I heard shots and felt as if my body and my face had been hit by a hail of bullets,' he said. 'I fell, and all around me there were the bodies of dead soldiers and my university friends, and although I was only half-conscious, I could see the officer in charge advance, gun in hand, to fire the final shot into the heads of the dying.'

When the officer found him, he put his gun in Moguel's face and pulled the trigger. 'Then all went blank,' said the student. 'By all tokens, I should have been dead. But I wasn't.' That last bullet had shattered Moguel's jaw but missed his brain. He lay among the dead for several hours until the soldiers finally left the village. When local women came to bury the dead, they found Moguel and immediately called a doctor. Over the next thirty years, he became a local attraction in his hometown of Merida.

Deserters

Historical records from the English Civil War record the use of the first firing squads. An eighteenth-century map of London showed an area next to Tyburn marked 'where soldiers are shot'. In 1743, 109 men from Lord Sempill's regiment, which later became known as the Black Watch, deserted in London after discovering they were to be sent on indefinite duty to the West Indies, but were captured on their way back to Scotland.

Three ringleaders – Corporal Samuel McPherson, his cousin Malcolm McPherson, and Farquar Shaw – were found guilty of mutiny and sentenced to death by an eighteen-man firing squad picked by lots from the Scots Guards on guard duty at the Tower of London. At six a.m. on 18 July 1743, the other deserters were gathered on Tower Green to witness the execution. The three condemned men knelt in prayer before being ordered to pull their caps down over their faces. The firing squad, however, was nowhere to be seen. 'What? Are we not to be shot?' asked Samuel McPherson. 'Where are the men who are to shoot us?'

The lieutenant of the Tower, General Adam Williamson, replied: 'If you'll kneel down and draw your caps over your faces, you'll soon be despatched.' When they did so, the eighteen-man firing squad marched around the corner of the chapel. Drawing up in front of the condemned, the main body aimed four to a man while six were held in reserve.

Above: A German firing squad executes an opponent. Firing squads were usual in the West under the Third Reich: hanging was the order of the day on the Eastern Front

The traditional order of 'Make Ready–Present–Fire' was dispensed with. Instead, a handkerchief was dropped as a signal, the Scots Guards fired, and the three men fell dead. Samuel McPherson and Shaw, however, still showed tremors so two soldiers from the reserve were sent to shoot them through the head. The victims were buried in a grave marked with a black stone near the chapel door.

Enlisted soldiers were not the only ones to face the firing squad. In 1757, after a chaotic retreat from Minorca, Admiral John Byng was shot by a naval firing squad of six marines on the deck of HMS *Monarque* at Portsmouth.

The First World War

During the First World War, 347 British soldiers were shot for desertion and cowardice. Many were young recruits, some suffering from shell shock. After 1930, the death penalty for desertion was dropped. There has since been a long-running campaign to obtain posthumous pardons for these men.

The French used mass shootings to quell mutinies during the First World War. The old Roman punishment of decimation – executing one in ten – was re-introduced. However, many received posthumous pardons and a token compensation was paid to their widows.

The United States army had a very detailed set of instructions for carrying out an execution by firing squad. The execution party – twelve men under the command of a sergeant with a pistol – and a prison guard formed up outside the location where the condemned person was being held. A band was also present and the main guard formed up behind these musicians. The twelve soldiers marched to the place of execution where they picked up their weapons from a rifle rack and positioned themselves fifteen paces from the execution post where the condemned person was to be tied.

The prisoner was escorted by the prison guard as the band played the 'Death March'. The band and the escort formed up alongside the troops brought in to witness the execution. The prisoner, prison guard, and chaplain proceeded to the post and turned to face the execution party. The main guard meanwhile formed up five paces.

The officer-in-charge faced the prisoner and read out the charge, the verdict, and the sentence. At the last moment, the sergeant tied the prisoner to the post and pulled a black hood over his head. The medical officer pinned a round, white, four-inch target over the man's heart.

The chaplain, medical officer, and prison guard retired to one side while the officer-in-charge positioned himself five paces to the right and five in front of the execution party. The order 'Ready' was signalled by his right arm being raised vertically, the hand turned palm forward, the fingers straight and together. The firing squad prepared their weapons by removing the safety catches. The officer then lowered his arm horizontally in front of his

body to signal 'Aim'. The execution party now pointed their weapons at the target pinned to the prisoner's chest. When the officer dropped his arm to his side and gave the order 'Fire', the twelve marksmen opened fire simultaneously.

The officer-in-charge and the medical officer examined the prisoner. If the *coup de grâce* was required, the sergeant would be summoned. He would shoot just above the ear, the muzzle of his pistol about one foot from the victim's head. Once the prisoner was pronounced dead, the execution party replaced their rifles on the rack and were dismissed. The band would play while the troops marched off to the parade ground. Meanwhile the officer-in-charge would lead the burial party and make arrangements for the disposal of the body.

The Second World War

Such firing squads were rare. During the Second World War, two American soldiers were executed by firing squad at Shepton Mallet, Somerset. They were twenty-year-old Alex Miranda, who shot his sergeant and paid the price on 30 May 1944, and Benjamin Pyegate, who had stabbed a fellow soldier to death and was shot on 28 November of that year.

During the Second World War, the American army executed one man for desertion in the field. He was one of 21,049 other US servicemen convicted of being absent without leave. Forty-nine of them were condemned to death. All were reprieved except for Private Eddie Slovik, the only American soldier to be shot for desertion since the Civil War.

In the European theatre of war, desertion was fast becoming a problem and the military authorities were determined to make an example. Slovik, a petty criminal, should never have been recruited. A frail and timid man, he was originally classified 4-F – unfit for duty – but with the shortage of manpower in 1944, he was reclassified 1-A and drafted into the infantry. Although he was such a poor soldier that he walked through his infiltration course and had to be issued with dummy grenades during training sessions, he was nevertheless sent to France.

Slovik had gone AWOL several times in Europe before he was charged with desertion in the face of the enemy. He signed a confession declaring that he was unfit to fight, but the interrogating officer advised him to recant and destroy the document. Slovik was also told that the charges would be dropped if he returned to his unit. He refused.

At his court martial, Slovik pleaded not guilty but was convicted on 11 November 1944 and sentenced to death. He then appealed to the Supreme Commander, General Dwight D. Eisenhower, for clemency but his timing was unfortunate. Slovik's letter reached Eisenhower in the thick of the German winter counter-offensive of 1944 known as the Battle of the Bulge. In the grip of a crisis, Eisenhower had little patience for deserters and approved the sentence on 23 December.

On 31 January 1945, Slovik was marched out in the snow to a large garden surrounded by high walls in the village of Sainte-Marie-aux-Mines in Alsace, France. The walls had been lined with thick wooden boards to prevent ricochet from the bullets and a wooden post had been hammered into the frozen ground. A long nail protruded from the back of the post so that the restraints binding the victim did not slip down and allow the body to fall to the ground.

Twelve marksmen had been selected to make up the firing squad. It was reported that when one of them asked his captain whether he could be excused from duty, he was told: 'Not unless you want to take his place'. That cold morning, Slovik showed more bravery in front of the firing squad than he ever had in front of the enemy. A member of the execution party said to him: 'Take it easy, Eddie. Try to make it easy on yourself – and us'. He replied coolly: 'Don't worry about me. I'm okay. They're not shooting me for deserting the United States Army – thousands of guys have done that. They're shooting me for bread I stole when I was twelve years old'. Generally, there was little sympathy for Slovik: frontline soldiers believed that a deserter put his comrades in danger so deserved what was coming to him.

The execution party were issued with twelve rifles, one of which was loaded with a blank. This last detail was done only for the sake of tradition because the standard-issue US Army M-1 carbine automatically ejected the cartridge of a live round, but not that of a blank.

Slovik's hands were tied together and he was strapped to the post. Cords around his ankles, knees, and shoulders held him upright. Prayers were said before a black hood was pulled over his head. As the order was given, eleven bullets slammed into his body but none of them hit his heart. The execution squad were all trained marksmen and it had seemed unnecessary to pin a target to Slovik's chest. He was finished off with a bullet to the head.

He was buried at the American Cemetery at Oise-Aisne alongside ninety-four Americans who had been hanged for murder, rape, and other violent crimes. His wife, Antoinette, kept up a campaign to clear his name until 1974. In 1984, army veteran Bernard Calka was granted permission to have Slovik's remains flown back to the United States. His body now rests beside that of his wife at Woodmere Cemetery in Detroit, Michigan.

Harsher methods

The army had other, more horrible, ways of putting people to death. A prisoner, for example, might be secured over the muzzle of a gun that was then fired: he would be disembowelled and his body torn in two. A marine caught drilling through the hull on board HMS *Rattlesnake* off the coast of West Africa was executed this way. The admiralty condemned this punishment as barbaric, but the ship's captain received a royal pardon. Death over the barrel of a gun was also widely used in India to punish mutineers. Baccheh Saqow, who briefly seized the throne of Afghanistan in 1929, used this method to dispose of his enemies.

Another cruel method was breaking on a wheel. The prisoner would be stripped naked and tied across a cartwheel or the wheel of a gun carriage. He might be permitted to cover his private parts if women were present. A brief prayer was said for his soul before the executioner or his assistant began beating him with heavy wooden sticks, mallets, or iron bars. Executioners prided themselves on their skills. The blows were directed to inflict as much pain and damage as possible without actually killing the person.

The arms and legs were the first part of the body to be broken. The bones splintered into sharp shards beneath the flesh and eventually broke through the skin. Once the limbs had been reduced to a pulp, the executioner moved to the victim's pelvis. The genitals were maimed until it was impossible to tell whether the person was male or female. It was only after the pelvis had been shattered that attention was turned to the chest. Heavy blows cracked the ribs until the lungs and the still-throbbing heart spilled out.

The Mutiny Act of 1689 introduced flogging with the cat-o'-nine-tails. Sentences of up to a thousand strokes were inevitably fatal. The punishment would be carried out in sessions of 250 lashes with the wounds being tended to in between whippings! Even so, a skilled executioner could kill a victim by targeting the kidneys alone. If he survived this ordeal, the ointments on his back could prove fatal once they entered the bloodstream and, with broken skin, there was always the danger of infection.

Above: Japanese recruits use Chinese prisoners for bayonet practice, after the fall of Nanking (Nanjing), during the Sino-Japanese war of 1936. Such actions were officially sanctioned

A prisoner might also be sat on a 'Spanish donkey' (a sharp inverted 'V') before increasingly heavy weights were attached to his legs and his body was rent asunder. This form of discipline was used in the Spanish army and later adopted by the British, who renamed it the 'wooden horse' and added a head, tail and legs. Also used in colonial America, it was responsible for the death of at least one soldier in Long Island, New York. The French used a similar device to punish prostitutes caught practising their profession in military establishments.

Naval Punishments

In the Navy, those guilty of sedition, mutiny or 'indecent practices' were hanged from the yardarm. As ships were far from home for years on end, punishment was necessarily summary. Once the captain had decided on a prisoner's sentence, the ship's company was assembled on deck and other naval vessels in the vicinity were summoned to witness the punishment. The articles of war were read out, along with details of the charge, the verdict, and the sentence. A noose was put around the victim's neck and the rope was run through a pulley on the yardarm (the end of the yard supporting the top of a square-rigged sail). A signal gun was fired and the end of the rope was pulled, hauling the struggling, choking victim up to the yardarm. He would be left to die by slow strangulation as a warning to others. The last man to be hanged under naval law was Private John Dalinger of the Royal Marines on 13 July 1860. He was serving on board HMS *Leven* in Talienwan Bay, China, and had been convicted of attempted murder against his captain. This was the last time an execution took place on a ship of the Royal Navy.

Although not technically a death sentence, keel-hauling was, in most cases, mortal. The victim was hoisted up to the end of the main yard where he dangled by his wrists. A weighted line was tied to his feet and run under the hull to the other end. An oil-soaked rag was tied over his nose and mouth and he was cast into the sea. Old sailing ships were so tall that the drop alone could kill a man. The victim was hauled under the hull before emerging on the other side half-alive and upside down. Being dragged over the barnacles growing along the keel would have scraped the skin off his back and exposed the raw flesh to stinging salt water. The process was repeated two or three times. Few survived.

The penalty for piracy was hanging. Victims were hanged from chains at the low watermark and left for three tides to wash over them. The chains stopped them floating away. In England, this usually took place at Execution Dock just down from St Katharine's Dock, near the Tower of London.

On 23 May 1701, Captain Kidd was taken to Execution Dock in Wapping to be hanged. The first rope broke and he had to be strung up a second time. A heavy man, he would have died quickly. After the tide had washed over him three times, he was painted in tar, bound in chains, and put in a metal harness that would keep his skeleton intact as his flesh rotted away. The body was displayed hanging from a gibbet at Tilbury Point, where anyone sailing in or out of the River Thames could see it. The gallows had cost £10 to build.

In his book, *Methods of Torture and Execution* (1966), Edwin J. Edwin described cruel and unusual methods, based on the old punishment of gibbeting, used by a certain Captain Lowestoft to torture his one hundred captives. A series of round cages were strung up from a network of beams and cross-beams. The victims, who were suspended from rusty chains inside the cages, with the soles of their feet resting on metal spikes, had to pull hard on these chains to avoid getting their feet skewered. Around every victim's waist was an iron band lined with metal points which cut into the stomach with every breath. They were given nothing to eat or drink: even so, some prisoners lasted three or four days before they bled to death.

C H A P T E R   1 0

Modern Methods

Although executions in the United States now take place

behind prison walls, there are so many witnesses present that

they hardly qualify as private affairs. When Westley Allan

Dodd, convicted of a triple child murder, became the first

man to be hanged in America for twenty-eight years on 5

January 1993, the execution room in the Washington State

Penitentiary at Walla Walla had special windows so witnesses

could observe the proceedings. Dodd had fought a ferocious

battle against the anti-capital punishment lobby and had

elected to hang.

At two minutes past midnight, Dodd appeared at the top window of the execution room wearing an orange prison uniform. His hands were restrained by a strap around both wrists. Asked if he had any parting words, he announced that he had found God and inner peace. This short speech was broadcast via the PA system. Two minutes later, a blind was drawn down over the top window and witnesses could see the silhouette of the executioner putting a hood over Dodd's head and strapping his legs together. A second man put a noose around the criminal's neck and tightened it under the left ear.

A minute later, the red button was pushed, springing the trapdoor. Dodd dropped seven feet into the room below. There was no blind covering the bottom window. A reporter said: 'I will never forget the bang of the trapdoor and the sight of his body plunging through it'. 'The body appeared lifeless from the moment it fell into view,' said a second observer. 'There was no dancing at the end of the rope, no gruesome display.' Another member of the press noticed 'there was no violent movement or noticeable twitching'.

Other witnesses remembered seeing small movements in the victim's abdomen as he slowly spun on the end of the rope. These seemed to have been involuntary muscle contractions because it was not thought possible Dodd could have been conscious at the time. A blind was drawn over the lower window. Three minutes later, a doctor declared Dodd clinically dead.

Hanging in the Lebanon

In other countries, these grisly affairs are still conducted outdoors in front of a crowd of thousands. At dawn on 25 May 1998, 25-year-old Wissam Issa and 24-year-old Hassan Abu Jabal were publicly hanged in the main square of Tabarja (Lebanon), just twenty metres from the house where, two years earlier, they had killed a man and his sister while attempting to rob their home. A crowd of about 1,500 spectators packed the rooftops and balconies around the square. Meanwhile thirty protesters, many wearing black, marched towards the square carrying a banner which read: 'We mourn the victims of the murder and those of the hanging'.

The police guarded the wooden gallows that had been erected in front of the local police station and the canvas sheet covering the building's façade was removed just prior to the executions. At dawn, the men were led out of the building in identical white shirts and black trousers. With them were two hangmen wearing white robes and hoods.

Issa was the first to climb the steps to the scaffold. When the executioner tightened the noose around his neck, the victim went limp and collapsed onto his knees. Next came Abu Jabal. He remained standing even though his knees appeared to buckle. Neither man was hooded or pinioned. When the executioner released the trapdoor, Abu Jabal dropped four feet but Issa managed to remain teetering on the edge so the hangman had to give him a firm push. With their feet nearly touching the ground, both men writhed in agony so the executioner gave the ropes a sharp tug to make sure the nooses were fully tightened. Crowds of people came forward to view the lifeless bodies which were left hanging for an hour.

Under the Taliban in Afghanistan, the pick-up truck used to transport prisoners to Kabul's soccer stadium was used as a means of execution just as the cart and horse had been used at Tyburn centuries before. Nooses were tied to the top of the goal posts and the condemned were made to stand on the back of the truck. The vehicle drove away, leaving them suspended. These kinds of public executions were usually performed with a bullet to the back of the head.

Five flat-bed recovery trucks were used in the public execution of Fariba Tajiani-Emamqoli. The thirty-year-old woman and her four male accomplices were taken to waste ground in the Tehran suburb of Khak e-Sefid at dawn on 19 March 2001 and sentenced to death for drug trafficking. Led out in front of a baying crowd, Fariba begged for her life but her pleas fell on deaf ears. The five individuals were blindfolded, their were hands tied behind their backs, and they were each placed on the rear of a recovery truck. Green nylon rope was tied to the yellow crane jibs. As the noose was put around her neck and tightened behind the right ear, Fariba told her executioner: 'May God forgive me'. The cranes were then raised, tightening the ropes and

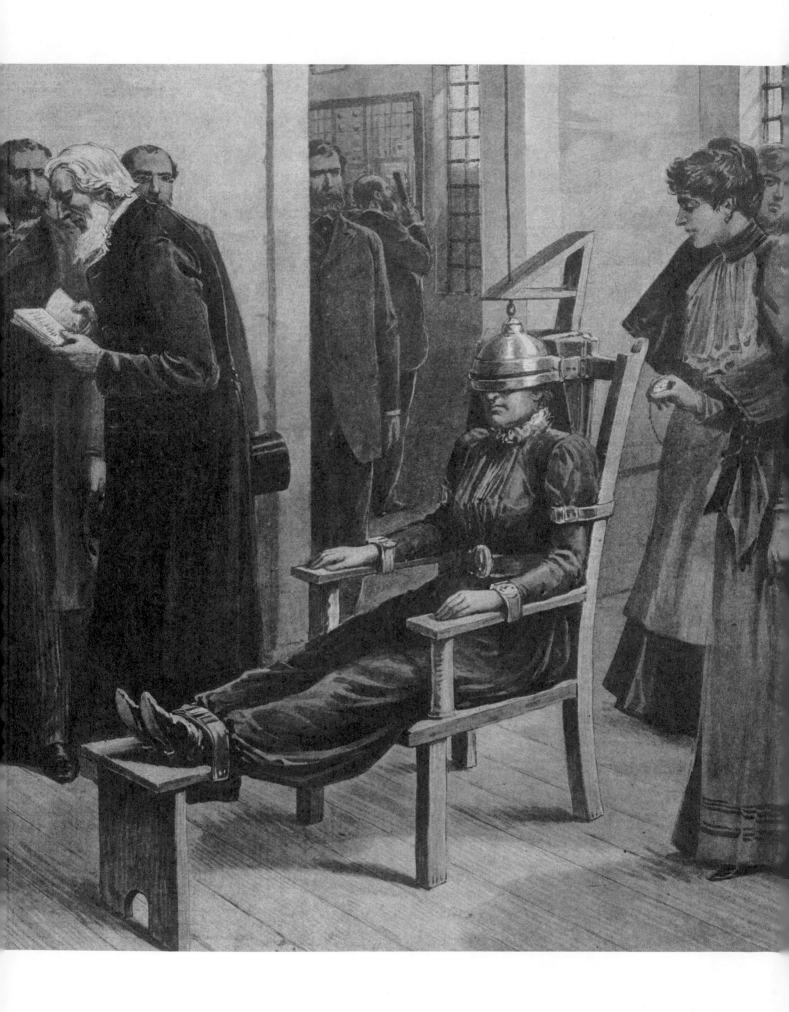

lifting the feet of the prisoners from the backs of the trucks. They struggled and kicked for about ten minutes before choking to death in front of a crowd of about 500 men, women, and children who cried, 'death to traffickers'.

More disturbingly, on 15 August 2004, sixteen-year-old Atefeh Rajabi was publicly hanged in the town square of Neka in northern Iran for engaging in 'acts incompatible with chastity' – having sex with her boyfriend. He received one hundred lashes. The judge became involved in the case beyond the call of duty, taking the matter to the Supreme Court, then personally putting the noose around the girl's neck – it was believed the girl had deeply annoyed him by removing her headscarf in court. Pleading for mercy, she repeatedly shouted 'repentance' which, under Shari'ah law, was supposed to afford her an immediate stay from execution. Even so the judge gave the order to go ahead with the hanging and later commented that 'society had to be kept safe from acts against public morality'. The girl's body was left hanging from the crane for a considerable time as a warning to others.

It is, of course, possible to survive the 'short-drop' execution. An Iranian man called Niazali was hanged in February 1996 but survived after being cut down twenty minutes later. He told the Iranian daily newspaper *Kayhan* that 'the first second seemed to last a thousand years. I could feel my arms and legs jerking out of control. Strung there on the gallows in the dark, I tried to fill my lungs with air but they felt like crumpled plastic bags'. The victim's family pardoned him. Under Shari'ah law, they have the power to grant pardon even after the execution has begun. Another man in Iran named Ramin Tshaharleng survived hanging for four minutes on 16 November 2001 as he, too, was pardoned in time.

The Electric Chair

Executions in the USA had traditionally been carried out by hanging. In 1886, however, the New York State Legislature established a commission to examine the options for capital punishment, and to investigate whether there was a more humane alternative to hanging. The grounds for this were that, on occasion, hanging could be very disturbing for the victim, the executioner and witnesses alike, and was also very often botched (see Chapter 4 pages 87–91 for examples of this).

At the same time, the nascent electricity industry was riven by the battle between Thomas Edison's DC system, and the newer, cheaper AC system developed by George Westinghouse. In an effort to prove that Westinghouse's system was far more dangerous than his own DC system, Edison organized a demonstration at his laboratory in New Jersey, where he killed a number of animals by the use of AC current. This so impressed the assembled journalists that the event was widely reported, and the word 'electro-cution' coined to describe it.

Facing page: Martha Place becomes the first woman to die in the electric chair, on 20 March, 1899. Witnesses recorded that the execution went 'without a hitch'

A further series of demonstrations by Edison's employee Harold Brown convinced the commission that death by AC electricity was both quick and painless. In 1888 electrocution became the legal execution method of New York State, and in March 1889 the first generators were supplied to New York prisons. (They were supplied by Edison, as Westinghouse refused to sell generators for that purpose.) All that remained now was to test the new method of death on a human. When William Kemmler was convicted and sentenced to death in May 1889 for the axe murder of his lover, the stage was set: Kemmler would become the first person in history to suffer execution in the electric chair.

The execution took place on 6 August 1890, and all did not quite go according to plan: the first application for seventeen seconds failed to kill him, leaving him unconscious, but still breathing. As embarrassed prison officials jolted him again, this time for seventy seconds, Kemmler thrashed around in convulsions, tearing his feet free of the restraints as the electrodes seared his head and arms. Witnesses reported the room 'filling with the stench of burnt flesh', and some fainted, while others fled the scene. The killing took eight minutes, and Westinghouse commented acidly: 'they would have done better with an axe'.

Despite this setback, and perhaps because they had invested too much in the new technology to abandon it, New York persisted in the use of the electric chair, to be joined by other states across America. The process was refined to eliminate the burning, but doubts persisted as to the painlessness of the procedure, and by the early twenty-first century, most states had

Below: Chechen separatists bring back the firing squad as a method of execution, 2003

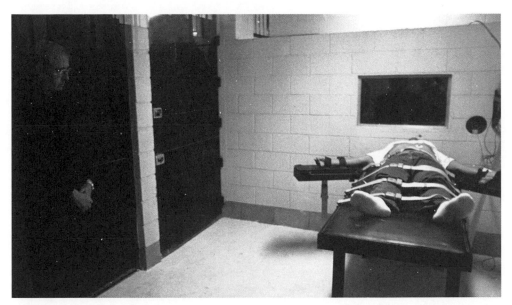

adopted the lethal injection method on humanitarian grounds. Only in Nebraska does the electric chair remain the sole method of execution.

Lethal Injection

Death by lethal injection is considered today's most humane method of execution. Introduced to Oklahoma in 1977, it is now used in thirty-seven of America's fifty states and also in Guatemala, Thailand, and the Philippines. An automated system is used and a computer regulates the amount of poison that is pumped into the victim's veins via a series of plungers. The switch that initiates the procedure is duplicated so that neither of the two operators involved actually knows who is responsible for the death. Medical ethics prevent doctors from participating although a medical practitioner must be present to verify the exact moment of death.

The prisoner is laid on a hospital trolley and held down by leather straps. A heart monitor is attached to the skin and two needles are inserted into usable veins. One of them is a back-up in case things go wrong. The needles are connected to long drips that run through a hole in the wall to the control unit. A harmless saline solution is first administered to the individual. Then, at the warden's signal, a curtain is raised so that witnesses in the adjoining room can see the execution take place.

A powerful anaesthetic called sodium thiopental puts the prisoner to sleep before pancuronium bromide or pavulon paralyzes the muscles and stops respiration. Finally, potassium chloride arrests the heart. Unconscious by now, the prisoner dies from asphyxiation and cardiac arrest. As many hardened criminals have a drug habit, it is sometimes difficult to locate a prominent vein. In March 1985, it took the execution team forty minutes to insert the needles. Death by lethal injection is neither painless nor dignified and, with so many people watching, it is still a very public execution.

Bibliography

The Book of Execution: an Encyclopedia of Methods of Judicial Execution, Geoffrey Abbott, Headline, London, 1994

The Book of Executions, James Bland, Warner, London, 1993

The Common Hangman: English and Scottish Hangmen Before the Abolition of Public Executions, James Bland, Henry, Hornchurch, 1984

The County Hanging Town: Trials, Executions and Imprisonment at Lancaster Castle, Dan Sailor, Challenge, Lancaster, 1994

The Encyclopedia of Capital Punishment by Mark Grossman, ABC-CLIO, Santa Barbara, California, 1998

Execution: a Guide to the Ultimate Penalty, Geoffrey Abbott, Summersdale, Chichester, 2005

The Executioner Always Chops Twice: Ghastly Blunders on the Scaffold, Geoffrey Abbott, Summersdale, Chichester, 2002

Executioner: the Chronicles of a Victorian Hangman, Stewart P. Evans, Sutton, Stroud, 2004

Executions 1601-1926: When, Where, Why, How, Who? – All the Principal Executions for 400 Years, Sungolf Plus Leisure Ltd, London, 1979

Executions and the British Experience from the 17th to the 20th Century, ed. William B. Thesing, McFarland, Jefferson, North Carolina, 1990

Family of Death, Geoffrey Abbott, Hale, London, 1995

Guillotine: the Timbers of Justice, Robert Frederick Opie, Sutton, Stroud, 2003

Hanged at Lincoln 1716-1961, N.V. Gagen, (self published), Welton, 1998

Hangmen of England: A History of Execution from Jack Ketch to Albert Pierrepoint, Brian J. Bailey, W.H. Allen, London 1989

The Hangmen of England: How They Hanged and Whom They Hanged – the Life Story of 'Jack Ketch' through Two Centuries, Horace Bleackley, EP Publishing, Wakefield, 1976

The heroes of the guillotine and gallows, or, The awful adventures of Askem, Smith and Calcraft, the three rival hangmen of York Castle, Stafford Gaol and Newgate, and Sanson, the executioner of Paris, with his cabinet of murderer's curiosities, full of astonishing disclosures concerning their private and public lives, and startling incidents before and after the performance of their dreadful office, Broadsheet King, London, 1975

The Reign of Terror in France: Jean-Baptiste Carrier and the Drownings at Nantes, Josh Brooman, Longman Resources Unit, York, 1986

Tyburn: London's Fatal Tree, Alan Brooke and David Brandon, Sutton, Stroud 2004

Index